A Year in a Small Garden

Frances Tophill

To Megan and Jo (Karen),
both dear friends, sadly lost
this year.

A Year in a Small Garden

Frances Tophill

Gardeners' World

BBC BOOKS

Introduction:

Journey to the House

Buying a house is something I never thought I would do. I'm a little unusual in that my journey as I meandered through my twenties and early thirties was broadcast, in part, on television. Many people who have followed that journey will have noticed that I have yo-yoed between different locations over the years.

I grew up on the Kent coast, and have a deep, pervasive love for the scenery of my youth, with its bleak, open marshes, cobbled coastline, bluebell-filled woodland, chalky cliffs and downs, as well as its chequered maritime history, mines, fishing, and biting easterly winds. But much as I loved this place as a youth (and still do), I couldn't wait to leave. Nowadays this corner of coastline, with its arcades, chippies and bags of higgledy-piggledy character, is the scene of many a second home. But when I was growing up it was down on its luck, the mining and fishing being mostly industries of former days, and full of seedy old pubs full of seedy old men: not a place a young woman particularly wants to get trapped in. I left school with no idea what to do; as a very dyslexic pupil, I knew I could never study history, which I loved, because of its reliance on reading. So I worked in shops. I did a brief stint of jewellery-making at art college, and pottery in my free time, and I sketched with my mum in fields and walked for hours on end. So when a job came up as an apprentice gardener, in a little-known Lutyens garden called The Salutation, I decided to go for it. Having never gardened in my life, I decided that combining creativity, playing with mud, and being outdoors all the time could be alright. I thought I'd be a garden designer, but in fact I fell head over heels in love with plants.

After a couple of years learning the basics as an apprentice, I decided to learn more about plants. Eventually I was lucky enough to get a place at SRUC – a university of agriculture in Edinburgh, to study horticulture with plantsmanship at the Royal Botanic Garden in Edinburgh. So off I went to Scotland. And I loved it. I loved plants

even more as I got to understand and meet more of them. I loved the lectures (pretty much full time five days a week – which was amazing); I loved my lecturers, especially Phil Lusby and Greg Kenicer, who brought the world of plants to life in studying their history, evolution and movements around the globe. I made amazing and lifelong friends, I learned about community movements in gardening for the first time, which have gone on to shape my gardening career profoundly, and I loved the landscape and culture of Scotland.

It was also during this time that me and a few of my friends went on a jolly to London, to have the bizarre and slightly terrifying experience of doing a screen test for a TV series called *Love Your Garden* with Alan Titchmarsh. This too would go on to change my life: a phone call a couple of months later, informing me that the job was mine, meant the last two years of my degree were spent juggling essays and exams with train trips down south and filming garden makeovers. It was an exciting and surreal time.

Life and work after university took me down to Devon. I worked in a market garden and nursery with vulnerable adults and a garden maintenance firm with people struggling with mental illness. Zero-hours jobs made balancing a chaotic and increasingly busy filming schedule possible – but my hopes of getting a mortgage less so. However, when you're 25 you don't really worry about these kinds of things.

So you see that my heart and sense of belonging was now split between Kent and my family, Scotland and my friends, and the south west and my work — and a landscape that I was falling more and more in love with.

I moved between the three places, both physically and emotionally, and have done so consistently over the years. I am not alone in this. Many of my friends are similarly torn. We are encouraged to leave home at the earliest convenience and explore – go travelling, go to uni, move to the city and so on. But many of us can feel a little displaced after all of this movement. My family did not have high expectations for me, and I am grateful that most of the pressure I felt to live an exciting, exploratory life came from myself!

I say all this because I think that sometimes the perception of a TV presenter (which is the most well-known string I have to my bow,

although I consider myself to be a gardener first and foremost) is of someone who has everything sorted out. Someone who's successful and together and settled. Of course, the reality is that it isn't nearly as well paid as people think, mainly because the work is only occasional and unreliable. So, like most other people of my age, I had to rent with friends, house share, and - for three years - move back in with my mum. I worked in large private gardens to enable me to save enough for a deposit on my first home, which (eeny meeny miny moe . . .) ended up being in Devon, mainly because that's where I got a 'proper' job.

Like many people, the pandemic threw me a curveball. I had just broken the apron strings (again) and moved into my own rented place back in Kent, in Folkestone, where my dad lives, when lockdown hit. I lost nearly all my work, as no TV programmes could be made unless I filmed myself on my phone – which luckily sometimes happened. I had to move out of my house, because I couldn't afford the rent, and back in with my mum (for the third time) and start applying for jobs. The first one I got was in Devon, doing tree conservation on Dartmoor, so I came back to the south west, and am glad to say I now feel very settled here.

I had the beginnings of a house deposit after years spent living with my mum, but to help me save more after moving to Devon, I stayed with friends. And so I started house-hunting, along with seemingly thousands of others who, after some Covid-induced soul-searching, decided to move away from cities. I booked myself on numerous viewings with hundreds of other people, went into sealed bid exchanges (something I knew about from friends in Scotland but was new to in England), and more than once wondered whether I should just buy a field and see if I could get away with living in a tent on it. But eventually, after two long years, I found a lovely couple who took a punt on me despite higher offers, and got my home. And guess what – it had a garden!

I've rented places with small yards. I've had an allotment here in Devon for a few years, and had a huge unwieldy allotment in Kent, and have shared allotments with friends. But never before have I had my very own piece of ground, modest though it may be. And needless to say, I have been very excited to get started in creating my first garden. Trees I've carted around in pots for years might finally, like me, be able to put down roots.

26 April
(wild garlic flowers opening)

Greenhouse. It's up! Well, nearly up.
What is up is its skeleton, and it's huge.
Too big in fact. I was there overseeing it
on Monday but had to go to work on Tuesday.
When I got home Rupert had gone but it is
really huge. At the moment it dominates the
garden. I knew I needed it done these days
because from now on Rupert is busy building
show gardens. But I kind of suspected I
hadn't quite nailed the position. Not
to worry though, as I now have all the
materials here to make it a little smaller
and even move it if I need to. The problem
is I think I might need to remove the bay
tree if I relocate the GH … Big job. Maybe
I'll see how I feel after a season of living
with it — or in it, as it's big enough!

PS I also planted a wonderful Mirabelle
de Nancy — that's one tree — think room for
one more!

Looking forward to delicious
fruit like this from the Mirabelle
de Nancy plum tree!

First principles of assessing the garden

When you go to look at a house before you buy or rent it, there is often very little time to really assess the garden. I went to the house three times in total before moving in. The first time was in the initial viewing, in late June, and the second and third times were after work in the autumn and winter, so it was dark, and I didn't see the garden at all. However, even if you don't have an opportunity to really inspect the garden, there are some basics that it pays to acquaint yourself with.

- **Size**
- **Access**
- **Aspect** (which direction it faces)
- **Presence of any real problem weeds** – I would include anything illegal like Japanese knotweed and also weeds that are impossible to eradicate like horsetail (*Equisetum*)

These basic analyses are fairly quick to undertake. The nitty gritty stuff like soil type, exact size, how the sun moves around, wet spots, cold spots, windy and exposed spots, private spots, places where you're overlooked, will become apparent in time. And besides, you're looking at a home first and foremost. For most people that's really the only reason you take this big leap: because the house feels like it could offer a place where you will be happy, safe and comfortable. The garden is secondary.

For me the garden was a huge bonus. My budget was very small for the area I was searching in and I was fairly convinced I wouldn't be able to afford a garden at all. I had started the process of buying a little house with a tiny patio about 1m square. I was really excited even to have that, until the survey showed the little cottage was in need of huge amounts of structural repair that I couldn't afford, so sadly I had to pull out. I say sadly, but the day I made that decision my house came on the market for the third time. I was so excited because I'd missed it when it had come up before and I'd been amazed that something like that – a house with an actual, real life garden – had been within my budget.

I finally moved in in February, full of anxiety and excitement, ready to start work on my first garden.

The garden I inherited in a nutshell

In terms of those key observations I advised everyone to make when they visit their new home this is how my new garden fared:

- Size — 9x10m — wider than long
- Access — through a shared alleyway
- Aspect — east-facing
- Problem weeds — none obvious except a small bamboo sucker coming up behind the pond, and noteworthy ivy climbing the neighbour's wall that will need cutting down some way once the nesting season is over

The existing pond with a tell-tale bamboo, which at this point seemed innocuous

A beast of a wood store. The structure dominates and shades this corner of the garden. I will either improve it or remove it in time.

Original garden layout

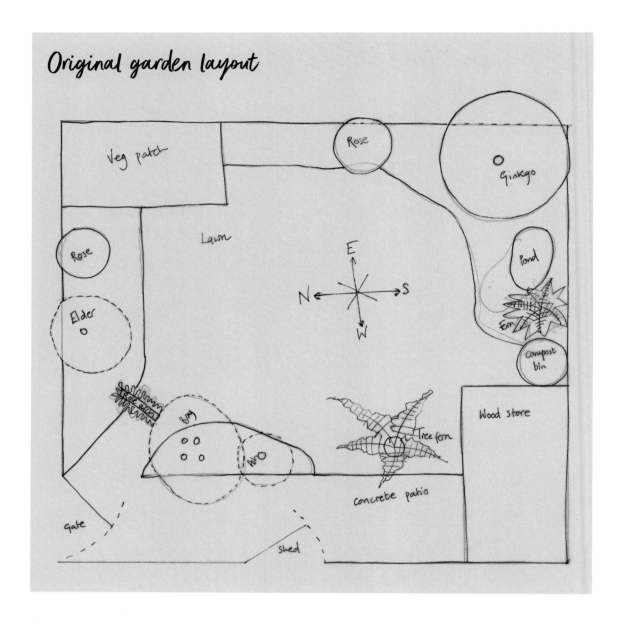

Here are some other observations I made while in the mode of assessing and beginning to think about what I might do with the garden. I recommend everyone think about these things – including considering the kind of garden you'd like to create. If you're not planning on having any plants then soil doesn't really matter but access does all the more, because you'll need to bring in hard landscape materials. But more holistic considerations like the feel of the garden, the warmth, where you find yourself being drawn to and where you find yourself moving through, can all help you to form the essence of what your garden might become in time.

Light

The first thing I noticed was a huge wall that entirely blocked out my sunlight. I think from March/April to October/November I have sunlight – though as I write this I am yet to see it disappear for the winter, so that's a bit of a guess. For the winter months the sun is low and won't manage to peep over that big wall. So light levels are something to consider.

I had spent a long time on satellite maps online working out the aspect so I knew the garden was east-facing, and that it wouldn't be the brightest for that reason. Sunrises rather than sunsets was what my garden would have, but that was OK – I'm up with the sun generally so having a place to have coffee in the morning was a lovely thought. What I didn't expect was zero sun in the winter. But this is where getting to know the space comes into play. Since I moved in, I've spent a long time just standing there and observing. In so doing I realised that even in the depths of winter I would get a sunrise were it not for a huge bank of trees beyond the garden. I am a big fan of trees and have worked in tree and woodland conservation so would never wish them gone.

For me, the trees blocking my morning light were forgiveable – the wall blocking my daytime light, not so much! Having said that, the trees in question were Leyland cypress, famous for offering very little to wildlife and blocking light very well. So when, in the spring, the owner of the trees decided to cut them all down to stumps, I had mixed feelings of sadness and relief. Now in the middle of winter I think I'll get some sunlight shining in, but the view I have is of air, sky and a few buildings instead of the trees, which looked particularly lovely in the moonlight. Perhaps whoever owned them will plant something nicer in their place in time.

Soil type

My garden is dark, humus-rich and, despite being very near the moor, slightly alkaline. Most soil types in the UK lean towards the acid, but having grown up on chalky soil, I am happy with alkaline, though it can limit the kinds of things you want to grow – *Rhododendron*, *Pieris* and *Acer* will prefer slight acidity.

Views and borrowed landscape

My garden looks on to my neighbours' gardens beyond mine, so nice and pretty, including a magnificent magnolia. Looking beyond your garden fence can actually inform some of the key design decisions you make and some of the earliest purchases and jobs to be carried out – specifically around trees. If you are lucky enough, like me, to have a view from the garden that enhances rather than detracts from your plot, then great. Use that view to make the garden feel bigger. Obscure the boundary so that you don't quite know where your garden ends and the neighbours' begin. You could even frame particularly nice bits with some trees. If, though, like many, your garden backs on to another garden or house, so that there is a sense of being overlooked, then consider what screening you will need. Again, trees will be your friend here. And this need not be a bad thing. For starters, being close to your neighbours can be lovely and reintroduce a sense of community that so many of us are craving, but even if you do want to completely hide from the neighbours, the creation of an enclosed nook of a garden, covered on all sides by walls and trees, is far from limiting. It creates the ability to feel enclosed, held, and hidden. Tropical gardens, Japanese-style gardens, cloister gardens and the like really lend themselves to this kind of space. So you see that by considering this early on you might totally flip your garden design on its head.

RIGHT:
The soft, verdant trellis fence between my garden and neighbour's keeps the boundary and still lets in light. A solid fence would make the space feel smaller.

Climate

My garden is very wet. Having come from the east coast originally, and the seaside most recently (via Scotland, which admittedly was also wet), I am used to very dry regions with lack of water being the main challenge, so excessive water on the southern edge of the moor will be a new encounter for me. The temperature is considerably cooler in winter than the coast. Whenever I visit a garden, people always say, 'We have a microclimate here, you see.' And I have to laugh because I hear it so often. I have come to the conclusion that everywhere in the world is its own microclimate. And over years you get to understand yours. I know that back home on the Kent coast, there is always a week or even two in spring when the rest of the country is experiencing the first beautiful, summer-like weather, and we are shrouded in a thick, soupy sea mist. It happens nearly every year. These kinds of observations take years to build up, and

in reality they don't really make an enormous difference to the way we garden, but using this detail to inform your awareness of the space can be the deciding factor between one species and another when you're shopping for plants. Or it can completely shift your thinking altogether. My garden has done this for me. I am very used to working with a palette of Mediterranean-style planting – partly because I love it and have an enormous interest in herbs and herbal history, but also because I have always lived in places that are arid and warm(ish), with harsh coastal environments where those silvery, protected leaves have evolved the right protection from bright sun and strong, drying winds. Here, the prevailing south-westerly wind blows rain clouds over my head more often than not – although these rain patterns are changing, as we have all observed in recent years. My little town sits on a hillside, which means the air temperature is considerably cooler, and the north-facing wall in my garden means I get no sunshine at all through the winter. These environmental factors mean the palette of plants I need to embrace will be one I have little experience designing with. The temperate rainforests of the local area mean that palette could be one of moss, fern and lichen, or it could be one of rich grassland; it could be bog-garden-style, or tropical in feel, but hardy and frost-tolerant in nature. Understanding these limitations or opportunities, depending on your point of view, will really open up a world of possibilities in terms of the plants you are able to choose.

Trees

I have a ginkgo (now only a few metres high, but will get much bigger of course, yet is one of my favourite trees so can stay for now) and a bay tree that has got very big for its position. The bay tree either needs removing or reducing drastically. For me trees are such an important part of the garden and landscape. Take me to a woodland on the weekend, even in preference to a garden, and I'll be a happy bunny. My work is as often as not in conservation as well as horticulture, and I know what guardians of biodiversity trees can be. They provide homes for many species, shelter from wind and rain, food, nectar, colour, shade, protection from soil erosion, flood proofing with the amount of water uptake they can accomplish, and are the most permanent form of carbon storage we gardeners can achieve. I knew my garden was really only big enough for one tree, and there are already two here. But despite that I had bought two before I even moved in. A morello cherry, for the north-facing wall, and a 'Mirabelle de Nancy' plum, because I miss plums, which don't grow wild here in the south west very much, and this is a particularly delicious cultivar. In a small garden it is really important that you select trees carefully. Of course they should only get to the size that's appropriate for the space – another good reason for fruit trees, which can be grown on any root-stock – and they should also provide multiple seasons of interest. Flowers or blossom in the spring (for me this will always be open flowers that can be accessed by pollinators), fruits or berries in the summer, or incredibly ornate and attractive foliage, and if they possibly can, autumn colour: the ginkgo is butter yellow, the cherry will have an autumn apricot colour, and the plum will have some autumn colour, though I have not yet seen it. The fruit themselves make it a must either way though. I have bought my trees fairly small for budget reasons. But smaller trees do tend to establish and grow more quickly. (For more details on trees see page 122)

(For more details on trees see page 122)

BELOW:
Beautiful *Sambucus nigra* 'Black Lace' that I will keep. The pink flowers make pink elderflower cordial, and the berries are full of antioxidants.

ABOVE LEFT:
Taking the solid end off
the wood store to allow
more light into the garden
and make it look less like
a bus shelter

ABOVE RIGHT:
Next door's grape that
rambles happily along
my north-facing wall and
actually fruits!

The existing garden

When starting out on a new garden project, you need to consider the garden that is already there, the structures, boundaries and existing design that you will start out with. In my garden these consisted of:

- A wood store with kayak storage on the roof of it – now no longer required as my kayak is inflatable!
- A little outbuilding that is part of the structure of my house, filled with electricity, shelves, an outdoor tap and the boiler.
- The following boundaries: a trellis, a picket fence, my house and my neighbour's house (the wall that blocks the light) on each side.

You will also need to consider the plants that are already in your garden. Mine had lots of roses, including a rose arch that you walk through as you enter the garden, a little veg patch including a rhubarb, grapevine along the trellis that connects me and my neighbour, elder (Black Lace), and a tree fern that looks dead.

The general design, as it currently stands, features a lawn at the centre, beds around the edges, shrubs, roses, green surrounds, a slight dead zone created by the bay, paving, a tree fern and a wood store near the house. The path to the wood store creates a bit of a thoroughfare and could be used more effectively to make the most of limited space. There is a very friendly robin, some house sparrows – lots of birdsong, a blackbird (that sings the same four-phrase song over and over – nice for a while . . .), presumably some wildlife in the pond but unseen through duckweed, rats in the compost bin, and at times running in and out of my outbuilding (NB always lock that door!).

I love the overall feel of my garden. It very much isn't a blank canvas as many people find when they move into a new house, especially one that's just been built. This garden, and the house as well, has clearly been imbued with love, joy, creativity and all the warmth that a young family can bring. If I did absolutely nothing to it, it would still be a lovely space. But with a little extra planting, and a few features I would love and have always dreamed of, it can be something really special. Besides, the beauty of owning a garden rather than renting it on a 12-month contract is that, for the first time in my life, I have the freedom to take my time and grow with my garden.

BELOW:
One of the roses under assessment. I don't love the colour or know the cultivar, but this one on the boundary fence does produce hips, which I use in syrup and that feed the birds.

Making your garden look bigger

It is hugely common in a small garden to create a design with small borders around a central lawn or patio, as this maximises the open space you have.

There is good reason for that and if one of your considerations is, like me, a dog who likes to zoom around in circles, there is a strong argument that could be made for keeping this design. I would issue a word of caution though. This design will make your garden look as small as it is. If you can see everything out in the open, including the boundaries, which may be emphasised by a thin bed, then you might find the space less enveloping. Also – or I might say especially – important in a small space is to create a notion of adventure and exploration. Creating planting or structural features in the middle or encroaching into that central area obscures what's around the corner. Yes, there may only be more of the same and not very much of it once you do actually explore, but it's amazing how the eye can be tricked even when it knows what it's looking at, and you can begin to inject a bit of seclusion and movement through the space. This will make your garden look and feel bigger. Trust me. Small features, and lots of them, exaggerate the diminutive size. The odd large feature, jutting bed, curve or obstruction to the view creates a sense of something behind and therefore the illusion of space, even if it isn't there. If you need a circle for zoomies or tricycles, creating a little circular path that cuts through these beds will make a trip around the garden really feel like an adventure.

Planning decisions

I'm a gardener. It's in my nature to leap
right in and get my hands dirty — and besides,
I had lots of plants that I was storing at work
which needed a more permanent home.

I knew I needed to get cracking. Far be it from me to be hypocritical, but I would reiterate: do as I say, not as I do. It is well worth making observations on light, planting, climate, warm and cool spots, wet and dry spots and all of those things for a whole year if you have the patience. Also, there is a lot to be said for taking the time to notice how you use the garden. Which areas you are drawn to sit in? Which areas do you naturally avoid? Observing what species use the space is also really valuable.

With the knowledge that I'd be sharing my garden with the nation, I had to make some snappy decisions. Luckily, if they turn out to be wrong, the joy of having a garden and intending to stay in it for a while is that I can always make changes as the years go by. That's the beauty of the garden: it is never finished, it always grows, and each year brings different challenges, so we, like the plants, must learn to be adaptable.

RIGHT:
A herb fennel – there
are some already in the
garden but this is one of
my favourite plants, so I'm
adding still more. They're
beautiful, incredibly useful
and beloved by pollinators.

2

Design

1 May
(saw first red campion)

Still pondering the greenhouse. I'm getting used to it but it's definitely too tall. Perhaps with chamfered edges, white washing, a lowered roof and some lovely soft planting, it'll blend right in. My friend Matt and my friend Mel came to advise me. Bizarrely the neighbours are OK. I'd be annoyed as it's right on the boundary but so far so good — as long as it comes down in height. In terms of positioning I think it could work but I need to really clear out all the stuff I know I definitely don't want — broken compost bin (AKA rat house …), big old concrete pots, tree stumps, lots of rocks etc. in order to be really sure the GH leaves enough generous open space to feel not too cramped or hemmed in.

PS Tree fern getting more and more croziers every day.

Hordeum jubatum – foxtail barley: an ornamental, annual grass to bring a quick, prairie interest

The tree fern, now fully unfurled

3 May
(bluebells out in full)

Perusing ornamental grasses in readiness
for a trip to nurseries a week from now.
Very exciting — incidentally also <u>very</u>
premature but I'll be in the area … I've
also potted on some of the edible grasses
and flowers I've grown from seed — barley,
oats + clary sage, verbena, echinacea.

NB — I must start making lists of what I
actually want to include. It's not a big
garden (9x10m roughly) so I can't overwhelm
it with species. Being selective will give
a more harmonious feel, and plenty of useful
spices, yet I still want varied produce and
succession. Must choose carefully …

9 May

Today I put in my order for my grasses
— along with some lovely perennials. I'll
collect them on Friday. It's beginning to
feel real now and very, very exciting. I
also got a mower from my sister as the cold
winter and leaky roof at work finished off my
strimmer batteries. So I can now finally mow
the lawn — which (despite the never-ending
rain in this unseasonably wet spring) is
finally beginning to recover from the film
crew spending the day here a month ago.
A couple of mud patches are still there
but it's the perfect time to re-seed them
now. Plus on Saturday I bought some lawn
chamomile from Mel. I'll try that too!

PERENNIAL VEGETABLE BEDS

This is generally done in the same way as matrix planting of annual vegetables, only in this method you tend to use plants with more height, such as perennial kale, Jerusalem artichokes, globe artichokes and many more. They provide a shrub-like layer around which smaller perennial vegetables or even annual vegetables can be planted. It is similar to a mixed border in ornamental horticulture, but instead of the more traditional flowers and shrubs you would plant large, woody, perennial vegetables alongside herbaceous ones which die right back to the ground in winter. You can even add some annual vegetables to plug any gaps.

FOREST GARDENS

This approach adds trees and climbers to mixed borders, all of which are edible. Trees like elder, apple, pear, plum, cherry, rowan, hawthorn or lime are planted with edible climbers which scramble up them. Climbers like *Hablitzia tamnoides*, *Actinidia chinensis*, hops or grapes can all do this. Around that you add a mixture of shrubby edibles like perennial kale or collards or herbaceous edibles like sea kale, sea beet, Good-King-Henry, rhubarb and asparagus. In any gaps, you can add annuals like courgette, chard, beetroot, garlic, onions, and even annual climbers like squash. This way you have varying root depths, allowing for plenty of root space so that roots can grow deeper. This reduces the need for lots of watering and keeps the weed burden down as the plants establish themselves to outcompete weeds. The most important thing is that by using this style you create a rich and diverse habitat with food, nesting, and hiding spaces for all kinds of creatures, as well as a feast for yourself.

Forest gardening is another method of growing productively but dynamically. It involves using trees and shrubs as a top layer and under-planting with entirely edible or medicinal plants to mimic the layers found in a forest. The only problem with this method is that not a lot of annual vegetables love to grow in the shade. The theory, though, is amazing: that the tree layer, shrub layer and understorey layer are fairly self-maintaining, as well as playing host to myriad species that will be in balance in the garden, eliminating the need for herbicide, pesticide or any intervention from you to control pests. These spaces can also look really as beautiful and need not be dark. One or two small trees, even coppice trees like hazel and willow, can provide the backbone. This means you have a crop – timber for stakes – and a tree storey that never gets too oppressive and exclusive of light, so you're not limited in the kind of plants you grow beneath.

I have always admired the potager-style planting scheme. This was invented by the French and developed across Europe over centuries, and is still very formal. The potager-style garden is a variant of a traditional kitchen garden, usually grown in raised beds, planted into symmetrical knot-like shapes and filled with vegetables in creative and beautiful patterns. They create a picturesque, and entirely edible, historic scene.

BELOW:
A golden courgette (zucchini) proving that colour need not always be provided by flowers – though courgette flowers are also bright and beautiful

My garden design

Although I am in the extremely lucky position of having the option to grow vegetables in the allotment and ornamentals in the garden, I don't think that is something I will be doing. My thoughts on that false distinction between the two should give you a clue as to what the garden will be.

In all the gardens I have ever worked in or had say over the design of, function of plants has been at the forefront of my mind and absolutely pivotal in the whole design. That has meant that nearly every plant I have selected has either been something I can eat, something I can dye with, something I can use medicinally or cosmetically, or something that provides a huge amount of value to wildlife. Nothing else has ever really been allowed to take up valuable space. Because I have the allotment though, which is purely functional, in my own garden I do have some breathing room. For the first time in my gardening career, my plan is to give some space to plants that for all intents and purposes may have very little function. That doesn't mean that the garden is going to be full of ornamentals, it just means I won't be limited by the strict restrictions I have imposed on my choices throughout my gardening career so far. In this space, if something feels like the right plant to use even though it may not actually have a specific function, I will not discount it. Overall the whole scheme will be filled as much as possible with plants that are edible, medicinal, wildlife friendly and useful in some way or another. I just have the luxury of being a little more playful here and paying a little more heed to form than I usually do. Each year I am intending to interplant the existing beds with annual vegetables too, and container-grown vegetables alongside everything else. Growing my own produce brings me an immense amount of joy and satisfaction, as well as the ability to cook better food, and I'm not going to give that up.

After all these assessments, all the considerations for the future and what I might want and need from the space, as well as what I am able to provide for local wildlife, I have come to a design that I think will work.

The hard landscaping

This will be minimal. I have existing structures and pathways that are functional. The patio by the house is the main problem in the garden, because it is laid on soil alone, and there are thuggish *Crocosmia* plants growing through the gaps, making the slabs very wonky. They lie underneath another problem feature, which is the wood store. It is large (larger than I need for storing my wood) and fairly unsightly. It dominates the space. These two areas are best tackled in one, but it might take me some time to work out how best to do it. The tree fern that I thought was dead came back to life as soon as the spring hit, and now the tree fern and bay tree combine to create a dead space right by the house. Dead spaces are something you really want to avoid when you have a small garden. Everything should be accessible and useful if it possibly can. The paving area, however, is also in the shadiest part of the garden. By 11am the sun has left this spot for the day, but I have to leave for work early, so it could still serve as a really nice morning seating area in the summer, when it gets the sunshine first thing. The solution I have come up with for now is to improve it by relaying the existing paving and then seeing what happens. I will revisit this area in future years and refine it to make it more functional.

Another hard landscape feature I know I want is a greenhouse. The obvious place for it to be installed is against the large wall at one end of the garden. That was my plan before I even moved into the house, but as soon as I arrived I had the (what should have been blindingly obvious) realisation that a north-facing wall never gets any sun, and so will offer very little warmth to tender plants inside the greenhouse. This has left me with a real conundrum. The next obvious place to put it would be against the house, so that it will get sunlight in the spring, summer and early autumn, from first thing to about 1pm. The problem with that idea is that it will involve a huge amount of work removing the concrete from that area so that the greenhouse can sit on soil, and I would have to rebuild the fence as that is where the entrance to the garden is. There is also the huge bay tree there, which would need not only removing but stump grinding. This is all too costly for me at this stage, and financial considerations are something I, like anyone who's just moved into a new house, have to pay heed to. The conclusion I have eventually come to is that I'll place the greenhouse against the fence, but further out into the garden. This is a bit of a compromise, as it will eat into the space and the lawn considerably. It will be such an important part of the garden though, and a hub for potting and growing, that I can afford this. Also, for the coldest months of the year this will be the sunniest spot, so it offers the best winter protection for plants. The risk is that I will be creating a new dead space in the sunniest corner of the plot. I can't put the greenhouse right against that far boundary for the sake of my neighbour, as that's where her seating area is and I don't want her to feel encroached upon, so I will have to get inventive with what I do with that little sunny corner. The added bonus to positioning the greenhouse here is that it will add a little privacy to the garden without it being too much. The garden is overlooked by big industrial buildings on that side of the plot, so adding a little height here will be no bad thing, and its transparency will mean that my neighbours don't lose any light.

Soft landscaping

The planting is where the heart of this design will be. At the moment there is a lawn with some limited planting around it. I have a fantasy of lying in the sunshine on a lawn underneath a fruit tree. I did this in a friend's garden last summer, and throughout my childhood, and decided that being able to do that in my own garden would feel like magic. So my plum and cherry will be on the edges of the plot with a lawn at the centre. I will go into more detail about lawns later in the book, but suffice to say for now that a lawn is infinitely better environmentally than paving or concrete, and also that my lawn care regime leaves a little to be desired, so in terms of biodiversity, there will be plenty going on.

Part of my idea is also to eventually let the edges of my lawn grow long. I can mow in the middle for seating and a table so that friends and family can share the space, but let the wilderness of the lawn come into its own and blur into beds that completely encompass the space. My lawn will create places to grow food and medicine, increase biodiversity, and borders in and around it will provide gentle screening to make an ephemeral hedge between me and the rest of the world, that will all but die back in the winter months. Simplicity is key here. Apart from a few environmental factors, like which beds are shadiest and which beds are sunniest, which might require small tweaks in plant choices, the planting will be consistent throughout the whole garden so there won't different beds doing different things, but one large encircling bed.

LEFT:
Devil's-bit scabious –
a native scabious that
grows on Dartmoor so
will hopefully like my
garden

BELOW LEFT:
Gatekeeper butterfly
basking in the sun

BELOW RIGHT:
Helianthus 'vanilla ice' –
a lovely pale sunflower

I have decided to try my hand at the prairie style when it comes to planting. This is something I have worked with professionally but not personally, and have long admired. Its ochre and russet tones perfectly align with my taste and with careful species choices there are plenty of prairie grasses that can tolerate the moist conditions, and even some that will handle the shade, though this is more of a challenge. There are some lovely ferns in the garden, including a tree fern, so the obvious choice would have been to explore this further and create a garden modelled on green, lush, tropical planting styles, but although this is a style I admire when done well, and can be incredibly effective in small gardens, it doesn't lend itself to the marriage of useful plants and increased biodiversity that I am after.

Many species that appear tropical but are hardy offer less function for native wildlife. And although some species like *Hosta* and certain ferns have edible spring growth, there are fewer edibles that could be incorporated into a tropical theme without creating discord. The prairie style offers the ability to really maximise on simplicity as the

lawn, which becomes more of a meadow as the edges are allowed to grow woolly, will merge seamlessly into the cultivated areas, creating a feeling of unification and cohesion. The hard landscape features will be nestled in the planting and the planting will feel united, with the lawn, meadow and bed indistinct from one another. It will be a mini meadow, a haven for wildlife, and a sanctuary and larder for me.

That is the plan for the first phase. I know this will take some years to achieve, and will very likely evolve as I get to know the garden better, because these kinds of plants need time to settle and grow tall and translucent. There is also a lot of groundwork to go through before I get to that stage of the project. I have to investigate the space, observe the light, organise the project and do things bit by bit – partly because of practical considerations like how much time I have and the funds I am able to access, but also because of the constraints of the space itself. There is nowhere to store any materials; you can't tackle two jobs at once because the garden will quickly become unmanageable with more clutter and waste materials than actual plants and space. Everything must be done in its place and at the right time. I have to accept I will be shifting and double-shifting and triple-shifting things around to make room for each task – especially as I am already falling into the trap of buying lovely plants when I see them, and therefore also already running into the trouble of figuring out where to store them until I create the flower beds.

It's like a Rubik's Cube, creating a small garden like this. Make ten moves just so you can get one important piece into place. It's the nature of the beast. I know there will be times when it might feel overwhelming, and who knows what the ground will throw up once I start digging in it, but if there's one thing I know about gardens it's that they're never finished. So focusing on the finished plot is never going to help you. The only thing you can focus on is the next step. Get that done and then move on. And one day, it may be in a year, or two, or ten, you'll get the satisfaction of having created something you love. It may even be completely different from the plan, but again, that's the beauty of nature. It never sticks to the plan we have for it.

RIGHT:
This is the first plan I am working to for this year. It's basic: keep the lawn, add enveloping beds and a greenhouse, then take it from there. This is achievable in one season and will get me exploring the plot so that next year I can take it to the next stage.

The plan this year

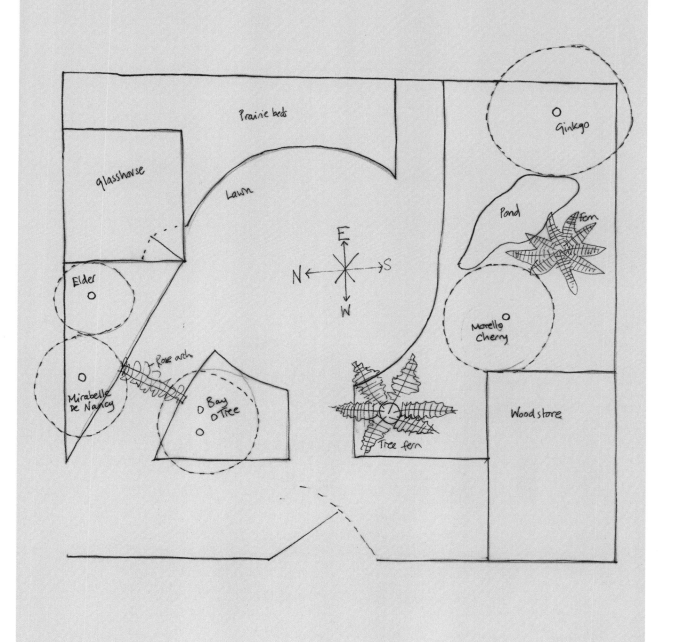

Prairie beds

glasshouse

Lawn

Ginkgo

Pond

Fern

Elder

Morello Cherry

E
N — S
W

Rose arch

Mirabelle de Nancy

Bay Tree

Tree fern

Woodstore

Inspiration garden:

Sussex Prairie Garden

This beautiful garden, created by Paul and Pauline McBride, showcases the way grasses and their corresponding herbaceous perennials can be used.

The prairie style of planting has traditions and conventions when it comes to how the plants themselves are laid out. Every gardening style has its conventions. In Japanese gardens, for instance, the style is so entwined with spiritualism that the exact placement of each plants holds real, sacred significance. In cottage gardens the groupings are usually clustered in threes or fives, or sevens in really big borders, with shorter plants on the front edge and taller plants towards the back so that everything can be seen. In botanical collections the groupings can be according to plant type, by region found, history of the evolution of the species, or just in order of the collection, to keep individuals distinct and clear – and clearly labelled. So the kind of garden you want to create informs how you place your plants.

The prairie style was honed in Northern Europe, notably by the Dutch designer Piet Oudolf, with whom Paul and Pauline worked in Luxembourg. The tradition with this style of planting is informal drifts. These are ribbons of planting that often flow diagonally through the bed so that wherever you stand you see the intermingling of the different species. The groupings are large, so that every plant has the chance to make an individual impact, with glimpses of another plant coming through, or catching the light in the foreground. In general, prairie gardens are vast. These large drifting groupings can work best on a large scale where you are able to see across waves of grass heads and flower heads, and off into the distance where something might very well repeat. This gives a sense of repetition, and in garden design, repetition creates harmony.

I do not have a large garden. It isn't tiny, but in comparison to the landscape-scale prairie gardens I'm familiar with, it is what I would call humble. So I have been wondering how to approach my planting. I am not creating a full prairie-style garden, as in this style, function is not usually considered much at all, and I want there to be an element of usefulness in the space I create. But I am mingling the lawn with the planting and the types of species I have chosen is very heavily dependent on grass species.

My question is, how should I place my plants in the garden? There are three options.

1. Treat the whole space, despite there being multiple beds, as a single bed that circles the garden, and place individual specimens around, hoping that the repetition through the space will create harmony despite there being no ribbon drifts. The risk is that with one of everything it ends up looking like a mess. Or maybe like a meadow, which is what I'm hoping.

2. Put all of one species together, so that there are different plants in each area, but big groupings of them so they feel intentional. This will work well in the autumn and spring when half of the garden is in shade all day and half the garden in sun, as I can choose species and groupings according to their preferences. The risk for this is that the garden won't feel connected as each space will be different.

3. Do something in the middle. Have a grouping of three, repeated in two areas of the garden, so it won't be a ribbon drift, but it will feel like an intentional cluster. This will create cohesion and look intentional, but will require buying more plants, and the effect will probably not be as unified as that created by option one.

I have been wondering about this for some time. I planted singly to start with, then I dug everything up and replanted in groups. I honestly don't know which is best and I didn't feel that either bed looked particularly well finished. I'll keep playing and editing.

After seeing Sussex Prairie Garden, where they have planted impeccably and used not just ribbon drifts, but huge, wide drifts to really beautiful effect, I have decided that option 3 is probably going to work best in my garden. Even in a relatively small space, I think the repetition of the species will be really helpful in drawing the whole completed garden together. I do not have enough space to make large clusters, especially of the bigger plants, but having a few together and then two or three somewhere else will create an idea that they are intended to be there and hopefully reduce the messy finish.

Some of the plants at Sussex Prairie Garden also made me rethink whether or not to include them in my garden. *Inula helenium*, one of my favourite herbs, a root herb used for chest infections and coughs, gets

ABOVE:
Inula magnifica – an ornamental form of elecampane, a root herb used to heal chesty coughs

OPPOSITE, LEFT:
A favourite of mine, *Sanguisorba*. These bobbling masses of flowers head range from pale pink to deep mauve. A relative of *Sanguisorba officinalis* – used traditionally to heal digestive problems.

OPPOSITE, RIGHT:
Grass seeds creating vertical lines and drama. Darker seed heads like *Molinia* or *Calamagrostis* work beautifully with softer seed heads like *Pennisetum* or *Deschampsia*.

so large there, and with such generous leaves, that I can see it would swamp my garden and reduce my ability to grow much else. It is also very bulky and doesn't give that translucence I am after. Whereas the species I kept finding myself drawn to wherever I saw them were *Panicum* and *Sporobolus*, neither of which are plants I have bought. I was also hugely drawn to the *Sanguisorba*, which I have bought, but have struggled to use to great effect in among other plants, so that reaffirms that a) I would definitely like to include it, and b) to include it effectively, I need to plant it in clusters. Plants like the mugwort that I grow as a medicinal, and the sorrel, which is an edible, are not traditional prairie plants, but their translucent and upright qualities will match really well once everything is established. I imagine it will be some years before I know if the scheme I eventually decide on has worked.

Another really inspiring thing about visiting this garden was the seedheads. I am planning on keeping seedheads on for as long as possible for the wildlife, and here they use seedheads to really great effect.

Maintenance in general is a really important part of the prairie garden movement. Staking is kept to a minimum by spacing plants that can support themselves alongside ones that can't. Dense planting, with growth most of the year, means that many weeds are unable to compete, and as you're not really touching and digging the soil each year, as with annual, weed seeds are rarely brought to the surface where they can germinate. The big cut-back, which you can imagine on a scale like this could take weeks and weeks, and might be really high maintenance, is actually very quick and commonly done using mowers or strimmers. Paul and Pauline burn their prairie. They said that in Luxembourg they would do this in situ, hoping to get a burn to quickly move through and take down all the top growth, but in the slightly damper UK climate, they have to strim and remove the dry material and then burn it in piles as often as they can to get a fire to burn through the beds.

Many plants can cope well with being burned. Some, like *Eucalyptus*, whose seeds won't germinate unless they've been exposed to fire and smoke, have adapted to rely on fire. Others really don't like it though. And all of them need a quick burn. Plants from the Mediterranean

ABOVE:
The eternally winning combination of *Rudbeckia* with grasses. Seeing this makes me want to inject some yellows into the garden.

OPPOSITE, LEFT:
Helenium 'Moerheim Beauty' always makes a striking display in the late summer

OPPOSITE, RIGHT:
Formerly known as Asters, but now largely renamed as *Symphyotrichum* (Michaelmas daisies), these flowers epitomise the prairie flower shape

OVERLEAF, LEFT:
Echinacea purpurea – a herb and beautiful prairie flower. These are glorious but temperamental; they often don't come back after a year or two.

OVERLEAF, RIGHT:
This pairing of Korean mint (*Agastache rugosa*) with fennel combines beauty and function in both species

biome (which includes parts of Australia and the *Eucalyptus* but also true Mediterranean plants like rosemary, lavender and thyme) have volatile oils that mean they catch light quickly, and the fire burns and then moves on. In a wet climate, the fire can smoulder for too long on the crown of the plant and damage it beyond recovery. In any case, I will not be burning my garden each year – for the wildlife itself if nothing else, but also because I am not experienced in controlled burns. It takes real skill. In wet Devon, it would be hard to get it to light, but in increasingly unpredictable weather, and sometimes extended periods of drought, burning can be very risky. So I will keep away from this method. Still, a strim each year sounds like a lot less work than many of the gardens I have worked in – especially when you consider less weeding and less staking to boot!

Clearance
Work

May — Chelsea Week

Life has got SO busy. It's that time of year. Work on the garden has really come to an end.

I managed to get the allotment re-jigged before coming away and seeds are sown so I can plant everything out soon, but even getting that done was a push.

And the weather has turned so hot and no rain for ages now. My lovely neighbours are watering all the flowers + grasses + herbs I've bought and grown to keep them alive while I'm away. I found them really nice cards here at Chelsea to say thank you!

The parched pots along the front of my house being kept alive – just – in the drought and rain shadow

June

Life is still so so busy. It's work
on the weekdays in the kitchen garden,
then when I get home from work, Zooms,
writing articles, or driving to filming
locations to film. At this time of the
year weekends also mean flower shows,
so there's little time for ... life!
The good news is I went zero hours when
May ended so am no longer having to book
holiday days off to go to work. I'm very
tired and needless to say the garden
hasn't progressed much.

I've planted one bed but keep re-
jigging it. I can't decide if each bed
should be distinct or if the garden
is small enough that the whole thing
can be planted as if it's one big bed.
Greenhouse still isn't finished.

11 July
Greenhouse finished!!

And STILL NO RAIN! The neighbours
are still being lovely and watering
whenever I'm away. Which is most of
the time. This is always the busiest
time of year with filming.

Bryony will get back to work in July and
then we're sharing the head gardener
job. Three days a week for her and two
for me. So fingers crossed then I'll be
able to really get stuck in. Also to
book in a time for Rupert and Dave to
come back and finish, slightly lower the
greenhouse. Once that's done I can get
on with planting up the garden.

The wood store

The wood store was the most dominant built feature in the garden when I first arrived. It sits in the farthest corner from the entrance gate, against the house, between the bathroom window and the north-facing wall. It's well built and functional but the reason that it is such a tricky feature is its size and scale in the garden and the dark corner it creates.

In a small garden there are always eyesores, because to build a big screen or fence in order to block off the functional features would in itself serve to create large, dominant, unsightly features that make the garden feel much smaller. This wood store is rather oversized for my needs, and has been fitted with a canoe-storing structure on the roof that adds to its already impressive height and creates a strange silhouette. I am unsure what to do with it. It does provide a kind of shelter from the rain, which there has been a lot of this year, in stark contrast to the drought we had last year. So it has its uses. What I do find is that it makes the east end of the house – the only end that gets direct sun shining through the windows – quite a lot darker. For that reason, I would really like to do something with it.

Eventually it would make sense to remove it altogether and rebuild something that's a more sensible size. The wood store stands above the only area of paving in the garden, and although that paving does need re-laying in time, possibly with reclaimed materials, it would make a nice place to have a proper seating area, especially when the sun hits in the early morning. Creating a proper feature here would also solve the problem of the dead zone all along that near side of the garden. It's kind of a thoroughfare, but in actual fact when you walk into the garden, the path under the arch of the rose is what draws you in, not the concrete path along the rear of the house. So a rethink of that whole part of the garden might be in order. To dismantle and rebuild a wood store, possibly as a multi-functional wood store/bench, as was my initial thought, would be a good job for a future year when I don't yet know what I plan to do with it, so I have decided to leave and just alter it for this year.

Having built lots of gardens from scratch and worked on many a garden makeover, it is a general rule that in order to redesign without compromise the best thing to do is strip the whole garden bare. From that point you can then begin to build it back again, in the right shape, with the right paths and beds and brand new plants. When you design a garden and build it all in one go, you want it to look amazing and finished on the day you hand it back to the owners, and hopefully, if done well, to get better and better as the years go on. In your own garden, there is no handing back, so you can just take it chunk by chunk, observing and reassessing as you go. Your own garden is never finished. I am aware, though, that it will inevitably mean there will be mistakes made along the way, and fudges to correct. If I were really determined to do it 'properly' I would rip it all out and start again. But I really like the existing garden, and it has plenty of useful features. The wood store, whilst big and clunky, will be a godsend come Winter. I am excited to see what the garden throws up as I start work. I also can't afford to rip it all out and start afresh. So, the design will need to be a slow evolution rather than a revolution. And as a big part of life is learning to compromise, it can't be a bad thing to approach the garden in that way.

Next to the wood store, further along the north wall, was a plastic compost bin – the sort you buy at a garden centre. Pretty early on when I sat on a small stump in the garden, contemplating what my plan for it might be, I heard rustling in that compost bin, and opened the lid in time to see a rat disappearing off inside a tunnel made in the compost. I have no problem with rats in general, but when you live in very close proximity to them, they can cause some concern. They can be carriers of the leptospirosis bacteria, which can be fatal or life-changing if ingested by humans, so best avoided. As a species I have no gripe with them, but in a small garden, so close to your

OVERLEAF, LEFT:
Glorious fennel flowers
that shot up from a
beautiful, tall fennel plant

OVERLEAF, RIGHT:
A healthy rhubarb plant
that I will probably
relocate to near the pond
in time. I love both of these
edibles though, so they'll
both stay.

home then it's much better if they're at a distance where they can keep themselves to themselves. My decision on this is to remove the compost bin entirely. It is really unprepossessing, and unavoidable, and if it's a home for rats it's something I can definitely do without!

Dismantling the veg growing area

As you walk into the garden, there is a small picket fence immediately on your left-hand side. If you were to walk along that fence all the way to the end of the garden, you come to the sunniest corner of the garden. This is where the previous owners had a veg patch. It is a really good place to have a veg patch, given that it's sunny. It isn't a raised bed as such, but there is a rectangle of wood separating it from the rest of the garden. As I have said, I would like to grow my edibles among the ornamentals, which means they might have to work a little harder in varying degrees of shade, but that can sometimes give a nice succession of produce.

My plan is to have the greenhouse in this patch, so the wooden edging planks had to go. This didn't take me long at all to do. In fact a morning was enough to clear the area. In terms of the planting, I can see some comfrey has appeared, which is a great organic plant food and known as knitbone for its amazing healing properties. However, it isn't necessarily great news in a garden of this size as it tends to be a bit of a thug. Digging it out is really tricky because of its deep, chunky, fleshy roots. This comfrey has a lovely blue flower (usually they're purple or white) so I was really tempted to keep it, but for the sake of having that extra space to grow the things I love I decided to remove it, in full knowledge that it will come back!

What I have kept is the fennel. Huge, healthy specimens of fennel are appearing in the area and fennel is probably my favourite plant. Edible leaves, pollen and seeds, great for hanging and drying, and gives spaces a curry-like smell, with lovely, ephemeral, yellow flowers that are lofty yet subtle, beloved by hoverflies. These, therefore, will stay and save me the money I would have spent on buying new ones! The soil in the veg patch is really dark, rich and fluffy, which bodes well for when I get planting the rest of the garden. In that area, there is an existing rhubarb, which I will keep but possibly relocate near the pond when the time comes, as forced rhubarb that grows in complete darkness has finer and less stringy stems. I'm optimistically anticipating the shade of that half of the garden might just have the same effect.

Removing the pond

The pond is one of the features in the garden I was most excited about when I first moved in. I am fanatical about ponds.

As a wildlife gardener, with a wish to provide for all kinds of creatures, a pond is indispensable. To my shame, though, despite preaching this message for many a year, I have never had a proper one myself. In both of the allotment plots I've had, a pond has been impossible – in the first because it was not allowed by the allotment association, and on my current plot because there isn't the space for a pond. There's barely space for me and my perennial veg! The only other time a pond has been on the cards was when I was renting a house with a tiny concrete yard, so I wasn't able to dig down. I did have a pond in a pot there, but for wildlife that doesn't really cut the mustard. So you can see that a ready-made pond excited me greatly. I was even planning on building the greenhouse around it to create a tropical pond at one point.

I was merrily working around the pond when a neighbour pointed out a small piece of bamboo growing behind it. This didn't really bother me that much. I can see where the bamboo has spread from: another neighbour a few gardens away. I didn't think much of it. It wasn't until the height of summer when I began to notice bamboo coming up all around the pond. I spoke again to my neighbour and she informed me that it had, in fact, been planted there, and instead of a single rogue runner from a few doors down, I had my own little thicket forming. So there was nothing else for it, the bamboo had to go. And in turn the pond.

This was unplanned and set back my planting schedule, which has become a little stressful as the plants in their pots that I probably bought way too soon are still sitting there! In the warm spring, devoid of rain, that meant a lot of watering, and a lot of help watering from my neighbours. And now that it is raining a lot more and I am here a bit more often, I am managing to keep the plants alive fairly well. But they're not thriving as they would be in the ground, or indeed, settling in and establishing. It's a good lesson for the future – not to buy too many plants too soon!

One of the main reasons for wanting to include a pond as part of the garden in the first place is the fact that they are so teeming with

RIGHT:
The unexpected monster of a running bamboo that was growing around, under and behind the pond and heading on into the garden. I caught it just in time.

life, attracting water snails, pondskaters, dragonflies, frogs, tadpoles, newts and so on. This hubbub of little beings is especially active in the spring, so that would be a really detrimental time to cause any disturbance. The first part of the task was to remove the large flag iris that had spread to fill about three quarters of the space. You should always leave any plants removed from the water by the side of the water for a minimum of 48 hours after removal, to allow all

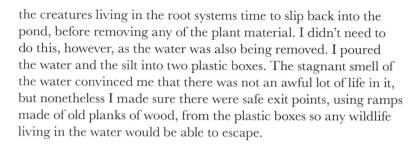

LEFT:

In the spirit of saving money and the planet, nothing gets thrown away here. These beautiful stones will come in useful around the new pond or in other areas, even just piled up as an insect habitat.

the creatures living in the root systems time to slip back into the pond, before removing any of the plant material. I didn't need to do this, however, as the water was also being removed. I poured the water and the silt into two plastic boxes. The stagnant smell of the water convinced me that there was not an awful lot of life in it, but nonetheless I made sure there were safe exit points, using ramps made of old planks of wood, from the plastic boxes so any wildlife living in the water would be able to escape.

The moment of truth revealing the soil beneath the plastic pond liner was hair-raising. It turned out the bamboo that I thought was just a few bits near and around the back of the pond was actually a network of thick, long, relentless roots, shooting out in every direction and forming a heavy mass beneath the liner on its search for daylight. These spears shot straight out under the lawn into a large chunk of my garden. I think I was very lucky and have halted its progress just in time. Another year would surely have seen little spikes of bamboo popping up all through the lawn and no doubt into my neighbours' gardens. Thank goodness I was alerted to its presence.

I afforded myself at least a day to remove all traces of these bamboo roots, but the reality was that the soil in the garden is so lovely and friable that I was able to easily haul on the strong roots, as if they were rope, and pull them out from wherever they were spreading to. The whole task of removal probably only took me three hours and I think (I hope!) I got it all. It might be a case of watching, eagle-eyed, for the next few years to see if any new shoots emerge, and dealing with them instantaneously if they do. An added bonus to this removal was that it gave me a chance to remove a lot of the crocosmia that has also spread around the garden. It is a lovely plant with orange/red flowers, but it has clearly become a bit big for its boots, popping up in every corner and spreading.

At this stage I was now able to completely clear the whole area along the north wall of all the unwanted plants, and begin working out where the design will go from here. I have a cherry in the corner (Morello cherry, which can cope with shade) and a ginkgo in the other corner. There is also a large fern. The plan will be to rebuild the pond, fill it with plants of a more in-keeping size than the *Iris pseudacorus* that was there before, and plant around it. Nothing too complicated, and very much along the same theme as the rest of the garden plants – edible prairie. But exactly where the pond should go and what size it should be is still to be decided.

Building the pond

There are lots of types of ponds and the style of garden you create will inform the kind of pond you build. For me, a pond is all about the benefits it brings to wildlife. Though I love the look of raised ponds, the most effective source of water and breeding space for all kinds of wildlife is a pond at ground level, because it is the easiest for animals to access. In order to make it safe you must make sure that as soon as there is water in the pond there are also exit points, so that any creature who falls in can easily climb out. A beach of stones also makes a really nice feature for animals to bask in the sun.

[1] Dig the hole. The beauty about creating a pond in this simple way is that you can make it any shape and size you like. Simply dig until you are happy with the dimensions. Generally, a wildlife pond should be at least two feet deep to maximise the ability for creatures to stay cool in deeper water. But, honestly, any water is good so just create something that your garden can comfortably accommodate.

[2] Make sure you have enough lining material. It goes without saying that you need to create something you can line effectively. Buy a really good pond liner (I like Butyl best – and each liner comes with a 20-year guarantee) and then dig a hole that the liner can line. Remember the depth and consider that in your calculations.

[3] Cushion the bottom of the pond. You will also need something to cushion the liner. An underlay would probably be enough, but, living in a slatey area, there are lots of sharp stones, so I am belt-and-bracing the pond here. I use a generous layer of builder's sand covered with an underlay. This will mean the liner is much less likely to be punctured, something the weight of water is likely to do if it just sitting on stone.

[4] Lay the liner. Like cutting out a clothes pattern with fabric this is all about reducing waste, whilst making sure you definitely have room. Lay the liner in the hole so that there is a little excess around all the edges. This will allow for sagging as it fills, but also means you can bury the edges once it's full. It will be creased, but as the water fills up these creases will be largely ironed out under the weight of the water.

[5] Fill with water. Generally, it is best to either fill the pond with rainwater or let the water sit for at least two days before adding plants or fish.

[6] Planting up. Choose plants appropriate for the position and depth of the water.

✳ Top tip

Start filling the pond while you're still laying the liner. Watch like a hawk as it fills and pull out any creases. The weight of the water as it fills will help smooth the liner and hold it in place.

Creating the first flower beds

As soon as the still-unfinished greenhouse was built it would become pressing to get the plants finally planted.

The longer they sat in their plastic pots, the more frequently they would need watering, and crucially, the less time they would have settling in over the summer to get established and spread out, flower and hopefully at least begin to give the impression of how the garden is progressing and coming together. It always takes a minimum of three years before beds really begin to settle and start to become what they will be in time, I think – therefore it's three years before you even know if you got the design right, and for me there is still more to do next year and probably the year after.

But as the months went on, still the beds weren't getting planted. In the end I caved. I planted the first bed, right by the greenhouse. This felt great, but also slightly nerve-wracking, as there was a very big risk of it getting trampled by us when we finished off the greenhouse. In that top sunny corner, where the vegetable patch had been, is the bed I have been most anxious to plant up, and most excited about. This is where the morning sun shines through. In an east-facing garden like mine, morning sun is crucial. Morning and evening sun are both magical. Midday sun is wonderful but dangerous to us, and bleaches the colour, whereas soft morning light is crisp and pure and evening light is golden. I get no evening light here, but I do get morning light and the flowers in the bed in this top corner are going to be the ones that feel the full effect of that morning light. I have visions of cobweb and dew-filled grass seedheads in the autumn mornings. I want to create a protective cocoon of delicate, soft, ephemeral dapples and shadows and shelter around the boundary of the whole garden. No light lost, but light enhanced, and yet a sense of privacy. This bed, therefore, is the bed that the morning light will illuminate from behind with its gentle rays, the crowning glory and the epitome of my concept. So I literally couldn't wait to get started and I planted it before I really should have.

A new way of planting

I ended up choosing a mixture of perennial grasses, herbs, flowers, pollinator-friendly plants and scent (which can be at its strongest in the morning, depending on species), and all with statuesque grace. *Stipa gigantea*, *Deschampsia cespitosa* and *Molinia altissima* were three stalwarts of the theme, and hopefully all species that can cope with the challenging light levels in the space. I will go into more detail about the plants themselves in chapter seven but the main principle of creating these beds is that although there will be multiple borders that wrap around the garden, they are being planted as if one. One that may shift, alter and undulate as it wraps its way around, but essentially, in such a small space, it's designed to be viewed all together. That means the traditional idea of planting in groups of threes, fives and sevens goes out of the window. That is partly because of budget, but also because I want there to be three, five or seven of the same plants overall through the garden but in any given bed, it might just be one.

BELOW:
A lovely *Deschampsia cespitosa*, commonly known as tufted hairgrass

ABOVE LEFT:
The grasses already
beginning to catch the light

ABOVE RIGHT:
Allowing plenty of space
around each plant so there
is room to grow

OVERLEAF:
The first finished bed at the
end of the season. It is a bit
messy with its gaps but once
it fills out it *should* look like
a riot – like a meadow.

For me this is a really new way of placing out plants, and tricky when planting one bed at a time. I have spoken to friends and colleagues and they all agree that this will make for the best overall effect once the plants have grown for a year or two and matured. I have to confess, though, it makes me nervous placing out a bed that has just one of each plant in it, as I think it looks a little odd. It is a challenge I have to overcome in myself. I am fully expecting to lose faith in the idea and dig up and replant everything in the more traditional prairie style of swathes and ribbons, as this will give the opportunity for unexpected moments where two plants work together, shifting as you move around and taking you by surprise throughout the garden.

Until I have all the beds placed out though, I will not know whether the current method has been successful. I have to have confidence and trust that I am doing it right, and the beauty is, that in a newly planted garden, it's easy to shift things around. And in a small garden, with not that many plants, it doesn't even take that long!

The Greenhouse

15 July

It's been raining all weekend so I started the morning by hanging my washing in the greenhouse! I used hooks and eyes to wire up the ceiling, which will be used for the tomatoes and cucumbers but for now they did beautifully for hanging my washing! Who knew a greenhouse would be so handy. I've used the washing line for cucumbers before but never had a GH to use for the opposite! I spent the afternoon planting the whole thing up. The toms are not looking too healthy having sat in two-litre pots for so long, but fingers crossed they'll pick up quickly now they're in the ground. Same goes for the gherkin. I've also planted pineapple guava and pigeon pea, and collected + brought back some plants from the GH at work, including peach, apricot and SA rosemary.

Clearing grass from the ground with Rua the lurcher half watching, half in the way!

[6] **South African rosemary** (*Eriocephalus africanus*) Used to flavour menthol chest rubs, and produces lovely white flowers in late autumn. It can be hardy but I have had mine die before so am not taking any chances this time.

[7] **Vietnamese coriander** (*Persicaria odorata*) – a strong coriander substitute with a spicy kick. It loves wet ground and a tropical climate. It grows fairly quickly but is herbaceous so can be cut back as often as you like, with the shoots putting on roots in a matter of days, if kept in water. So it's very, very easy to propagate.

[8] **African bulbine** (*Bulbine frutescens*) – used to heal burns in a similar way to aloe. I first encountered this plant when working on community farms in South African townships and informal settlements. This is the go-to treatment for burns there if someone is unable to see a doctor. It grows around the Cape, and has a lovely yellow/orange flower spike, very like an aloe.

[9] **Soap aloe** (*Aloe maculata*) – a large-leafed aloe used, like many others, for treating irritated and sore skin. As the name suggests, the mucus inside the leaves can be used as a substitute for soap.

✷ **ANNUAL PLANTS:**

I also have lots of annual plants that I have been growing in two-litre pots all summer and are now sulking as a consequence, including a few different tomatoes, and a gherkin. I also have some Japanese indigo (*Persicaria tinctoria*) which was given to me by a friend and is used in traditional Japanese dye-making [10]. I will collect the seeds from these at the end of the year and re-grow them each year. Later in the summer I am learning how to process the dye, which is an intricate process, involving fermenting the leaves. The good thing is that with strong dyes like this, using a mordant to strip the fabric of its defences is unnecessary. And indigo is a favourite colour of mine so learning how to process it will be a real education.

OVERLEAF LEFT:
The first view of the greenhouse as you enter the garden. In time, as the plants bulk out, it will be partially obscured.

OVERLEAF RIGHT:
Taro root is a commonly consumed crop in Asia. This is a purple form. *Colocasia* is the Latin. If I plant in the gound it will get above eight feet tall ... food for thought – literally.

5

Trees

12 August
Planting up!

I have finally started to get things in the ground in earnest. I have left it a bit late to make a real impact this year I suspect. Still, the grasses are largely in the ground, which means that they will have time to get a little bit established before Autumn comes. I went to a Japanese indigo making workshop the other day. It was AMAZING learning the traditional method of dyeing with water made from cooked plum tree ash and spring water — with a stirring method very like biodynamics — and a process that takes weeks to achieve. The fermented indigo then makes the most incredible blue colour. I can honestly say I don't think I will ever be able to achieve this at home. The time and love that went into this process was astonishing. I left with a whole new respect for indigo cloth, and blue fingernails! I also got a lovely 600-year-old strain of *Persicaria tinctoria* so I can save the seed and grow more next year.

Blue fingernails after my first attempt at using Japanese Indigo. They stayed blue until my nails grew out!

The first beds are planted up and settling in. I'm hoping they settle in well so that next spring they really come into their own.

The allotment in its full summer glory. This is the view of the evening sun from my little bench. I love this spot.

28 August
BOUNTY!

The allotment is looking so lush and green and full of produce. It's amazing. No matter how many years I garden, I always find it hard to believe that this bounty will emerge when you sow these tiny seeds in the Spring. Yet here it is. The *Tithonia* is about eight feet tall. The hops are out in full force and mushrooms are looking resplendent in the woods around here. It goes to show how wet it has been. They are so early this year! The sun has managed to come out a few times though. Now the plants are in the ground and *Gardeners' World* has done its second visit (a long, wet and slightly gruelling day — this summer has certainly been a wet one), I have relaxed a little and even got the hammock out!

Wildlife – a hugely rich and varied food source for all kinds of wildlife, these trees provide for myriad species including many caterpillars and insects feeding on their leaves, birds nesting in their branches, mammals, even large ones like deer, feeding on acorns, and insect-eating birds feeding from all the rich pickings found in their boughs.

———

[6] **PINE (SCOTS)** *(Pinus sylvestris)*
A stunning conifer that starts off conical but spreads to form wide, generous bows, easily distinguished by its orange, rust-coloured bark near the tips. The Scots pine has sets of two needles, which are slightly twisted. They can live for up to 700 years. Traditionally they have been used as a source of turpentine, resin and tar and the timber was used for making ship masts.

Wildlife – in native Scotland they can be home to rare animals like the capercaillie and red squirrel. Generally, they are really useful to nesting birds.

———

PLYMOUTH PEAR *(Pyrrhus cordata)*
Really only native to Plymouth and is incredibly rare, with protected status. Propagating it without a licence is illegal. Buying it from a reputable source, though, will not only provide for wildlife, but also help to conserve this endangered species.

Wildlife – the pears are not particularly good for us to eat, but the flowers provide nectar for bees and pollinators and the fruits are edible to many birds and mammals once they are ripe.

———

[7] ROWAN *(Sorbus aucuparia)*

A lovely, mythical and delicate tree. This is a great one for small gardens, as it doesn't get too big and provides lots of visual treats, including delicate leaves with red autumn colour, clusters of white flowers and then clusters of red (or other colours in cultivated forms) berries. Believed to keep out bad spirits and invite in good ones, the rowan is a tree of cultural significance in folklore. The berries, like many other rose family members, are edible to humans and have good immune-boosting properties. They can be used in jams, alcohol making and in syrups.

Wildlife – the flowers provide nectar and the berries provide fruits, which makes this a really valuable tree to wildlife. They can even provide a nice feast for often maligned deer.

––––

SPINDLE *(Euonymus europaeus)*

A really breathtaking tree. You won't notice it until the late summer when it produces its incredible pink and orange fruits. From then it goes on to produce striking autumn colour. When the leaves fall it reveals winged stems. It is an overlooked but very important native tree. It is meant to be a good omen – this is what the Greek origins of its name refer to. Legend had it, though, that if it flowered early, an outbreak of plague was coming!

Wildlife – the berries, poisonous to us, are eaten by birds and small mammals as well as red foxes.

––––

WHITEBEAM (ALSO ARRAN, DEVON & ROCK WHITEBEAM) *(Sorbus aria, arranensis, devoniensis & rupicola)*

This is a tree that hybridises easily, so small isolated populations of new species can be found around the British Isles. As you might notice from its binomial name, it is very closely related to the rowan. In looks though, despite similar flowers and berries, it is quite different.

If rowan is a fairy, then whitebeam is a witch. A white witch in the spring, with silver, downy leaves and white clusters of flowers, and a gnarled old hag from a Brothers Grimm tale in the autumn, when its leaves go, not red like the rowan, but tough, brown and leathery against its red berries. For this I love the whitebeam. It is misunderstood for its ugliness, but still bountiful and generous to the wildlife. And with the ability to speciate and adapt quickly, it can be found in remote places, like moors, crags and cliffs, providing for a wider range of animals.

Wildlife – like the rowan the flowers are nectar rich and the berries are good for birds and mammals alike, including to us when they are bletted, like a medlar.

––––

WILD SERVICE TREE *(Sorbus torminalis)*

Yet another native sorbus, only this one does not have red berries, but golden brown ones. It has acer-shaped leaves too. Another name for this tree is the chequers tree, and its berries were used to make strong beer, hence the name 'the Chequers Inn' for many pubs!

Wildlife – the berries are really loved by wood pigeons as well as the flowers being a good source of nectar.

––––

WILLOW (BAY, GOAT & GREY)

(Salix pentandra, Salix caprea, Salix cinerea)
Willow is a great asset to us and to the landscape. It is used as biofuel, as it is such a quick-growing tree, and it is a crucial part of many crafts including willow weaving and basketry, which varies from region to region, and even extends to include the now increasingly popular willow coffin industry. Cuttings of the whips can be taken really easily by just sticking them fresh into the ground, and they will take root. That means you can create living woven structures from willow. You will just need to prune it to keep it in check. The

willows themselves are great wetland species, need a fairly damp soil and in areas prone to flooding can be a great help in preventing flood damage and soil erosion.

Wildlife – willow are especially good for caterpillar and moth species. Goat willow provides for the sallow kitten, sallow clearwing, dusky clearwing and lunar hornet clearwing. The grey willow is the food source for the famous purple emperor butterfly larvae. The bay willow is a really good food source of the black spot sallow pigmy moth.

———

[8] YEW *(Taxus baccata)*

If you thought the Scots pine was long-lived then meet the yew. This tree can live healthily for thousands of years. The oldest we know of is the Fortingall Yew in Perthshire, dated at between 2,000 and 3,000 years old (maybe even older, according to some estimates). These incredible species are dioecious, meaning there are male and female plants. The males produce oodles of pollen in the spring, and females produce red berries. All parts of the yew, except the fleshy part of the fruits, are deadly poisonous. Even just six of the seeds found in the fruit could kill an adult, so treat them with caution. Nobody knows quite why but yew trees have extreme spiritual significance and can be found at many sacred places, including churchyards, where the trees usually pre-date the actual churches. The wood was used to make the old English longbow. There is undoubtedly a feeling of history and wisdom surrounding these amazing creatures. The American yew is used to create the chemotherapy drug paclyitaxel, used in the treatment of many cancers.

Wildlife – as one of the few conifers that can be cut back as hedging, it can make a really good nesting opportunity for many birds. The berries can also provide food for woodland mammals.

7

8

Trees in a small garden

Not all of these trees are suitable for small gardens. There is an inexhaustive list of non-native trees which can also provide a really good feature in small gardens, but will nearly always be less useful for the local wild species you share your garden with.

RIGHT:
This cherry is the second tree I have planted in the garden. Good for wildlife, beautiful and tasty!

✳ **A FEW SMALL NON-NATIVE TREES I RECOMMEND FOR THEIR BEAUTY:**

- Juneberry, *Amelanchier × lamarckii*

- Harlequin glorybower, *Clerodendrum trichotomum*

- Chilean myrtle, *Luma apiculata*

- Common myrtle, *Myrtus communis*

- Katsura, *Cercidiphyllum japonicum*

- Eastern redbud, *Cercis canadensis*

- Himalayan birch, *Betula utilis var. jacquemontii*

- Olive tree, *Olea europaea* (make sure you buy it from a reputable source that has quarantined it against Xylella virus)

- Kousa dogwood, *Cornus kousa*

- Common lilac, *Syringa vulgaris*

- Star magnolia, *Magnolia stellata*

- Japanese camellia, *Camellia japonica* (with a lifted crown and cleared lower stems to expose the trunks)

Remember that trees are a really important backbone of the ecosystem and provide an awful lot of shelter, food and protection for all kinds of creatures. Choosing carefully is important, and in my humble opinion making sure you include at least one in your garden is crucial.

Trees I have chosen

In my garden I already have a bay tree (which excludes a lot of light) and a *Ginkgo biloba* (maidenhair tree), which I love.

RIGHT:
Admiring the elder while trying to work out where to plant this lovely red hazel I was given

I think the bay will eventually go. It does tick boxes in that it is a useful species, but the reality is that I am not going to ever get through that much bay in my cooking and the exclusion of light is more important to me. So I will remove this tree and replace it with a purple hazel.

I will keep the ginkgo. I love the species – its use in herbal medicine for memory loss, and its ancient status as one of the first trees to evolve, makes it a magnificent specimen. It was not staked during the planting and, now that it has grown to peep above the roofline, the wind is causing it some harm. A rather heavy-handed prune to remove its unbalanced and lopsided growth might help. If it does fall down or lean more alarmingly, then it might be time to rethink and choose something else. But for now I'm going to see how it fares.

There is also a little elder 'Black Lace' here, which I will keep for its pink flowers, producing pink cordial.

The trees I have added are really very predictable. The first is a plum. A Mirabelle plum to be precise, called 'Mirabelle de Nancy'. It produces small, round, yellow skinned, but pink fleshed fruits, that taste out of this world when eaten fresh, but also cook beautifully. I tend to stew them and freeze them for a taste of summer all winter. Devon is not the best climate for wild plums so I am hoping that these will be happy here. The flowers and fruits, as well as the branches, offer a haven for wildlife. I have put this plum by the entrance to the garden. It is really important in a space like this to place the trees carefully so that they do not exclude light from either me or my neighbours. In this position in the south west corner, it should hardly shade anybody.

I am also adding a Morello cherry, and the reason I have chosen this is partly for its wildlife credentials (I imagine I won't get to eat a single fruit after the birds have found it) but also for its fairly unique ability to survive a north-facing wall and still produce fruits.

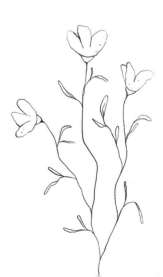

I am hoping I will at least get something to eat from this tree. If not though, I have the spring blossom, which will catch the morning light, and the autumn colour that will do the same. I love cherry's autumn colour for its soft peach/pink/yellow hues. Cherries also have a nicer form than plums so in time this will hopefully be a really good asset.

I am growing three more trees, but these are potted (five in the ground is already pushing it for any small garden!): a peach, an apricot and an almond. So basically all the additions I have made, except my hazel, which was given to me, are in the genus *Prunus*. Plum (*Prunus domestica*), cherry (*Prunus cerasus* 'Morello'), peach (*Prunus persica*), apricot (*Prunus armeniaca*), and almond (*Prunus dulcis*). This wasn't deliberate – in fact it's only now, in writing it down, that I've noticed it. I suppose the conclusion is that if, like me, you want to enjoy both looking at and eating your trees, and you don't have a huge garden, then perhaps the genus *Prunus* is the answer!

Espalier pruning a dwarf cherry tree

* **Top tip**

This job is best done in summer. Apples and pears and roses are in the same family, and are best pruned in winter, but cherries are susceptible to something called silver-leaf disease. This is much less likely to occur if the cherry is pruned in the summer.

[1] Training in a leader. I have had this cherry for years and this is its first prune, which will create the initial shaping of the espalier. The first thing to do is select a leader and tie it to the fence so that it grows vertically. This will become the central stem of the espalier and can reach the top of the fence, where I will snip it.

[2-3] Select the lower stems you want to keep and cut off any that do not add to the espalier or fan shape. Completely remove any branches growing forwards, backwards or in the wrong position up the stem.

[4] With the branches you do wish to keep, bend them down to at least a 45° angle, or horizontal (you can do this half way this year and then complete it next if you're worried you'll snap the branches) and tie them into position. Then snip off any stems growing from these horizontals and take them back to fruiting spurs. These are basal clusters of buds where fruit will grow next year. Make sure all your cuts (and tools) are clean.

Amanda Patton's garden

Amanda Patton is an award-winning garden
and landscape designer and I first visited
her garden some years ago when it was fairly
newly planted.

It is a really similar size to mine and although completely different in
style (hers is very modern, where I am starting mine as fairly simple
and low impact, in keeping with the traditional style of my house) it
uses many of the same species I am hoping to use and it is designed
to be very wildlife friendly. I therefore wanted to revisit and see how
it has developed and changed over the years.

I was not disappointed. The whole space is completely different from
how it was when I last saw it. It's really come into its own and has
become much greener than it was before. It has also become much
more private. Amanda does not have the same privacy concerns as
me, not having neighbours on two sides, but she is across the road
from a pub, so she has many people walking past and observing her
house throughout the day and evening.

She also has a garden of two halves, being half sunshine and half
shade, so it was really interesting to see how she has used that. She
has very sensibly put her seating area in the sun and the main garden
structure, which is similar in dimensions to my greenhouse but
completely different in material, in the shady corner. Her structure,
though, is not a greenhouse but an art studio. So there isn't the same
need for warm, bright space to grow plants in.

Just as I did by mistake, Amanda has intentionally left a small
corridor at the end of the building. She uses it for compost bins, but
her reasoning was that it brought the building out into the garden
and so it felt like an integral part of the space rather than being
shoved into a corner. It makes me feel relieved that a designer has
chosen this – perhaps it wasn't such a big mistake after all for my
greenhouse. I just need to make sure I find a use for that little narrow
corner!

Something I really loved about her garden was the beautiful bird bath right in the middle of one of the borders. I have long thought about bringing more water into my garden. I may run out of time this year to include something like this, but I think it will become the template for something similar that I would like to make. Perhaps I'll use a wok and some concrete (or alternative, as I am trying to keep my concrete use to a minimum for environmental reasons) and mount it in the middle of a border, where I can watch the birds bathing in it. The addition of some pebbles on one end will also make it a safe place for insects to bath and drink too.

The form of Amanda's garden is really to my taste, and in many ways much more in my comfort zone than the space I am creating in Devon. She has no lawn, which is more my usual style – I tend to prefer gravel and dry gardens, but it would be totally incongruous on the edge of the moor and the thought of having a lawn to lie on seems really lovely to me, having not had one since I was a child. Instead of lawn she has decking at the centre of the garden where the seating area is, and then beautiful rectangular pavers creating geometric paths that take you around the garden.

BELOW:
The bird bath, simple but striking form that adds weight and structure

ABOVE:
These pavers covered in planting keep greenery but add two things: useful, hard-wearing pathways and visual structure.

I have so far kept to grass paths, but am slowly rethinking. Seeing these gives me confidence to go back to the drawing board when it comes to pathways.

These are a real triumph, and were an unexpected piece of inspiration to me. She has wide gaps between each slab, and in these gaps violets, mind-your-own-business and little *Thalictrum* seedlings are allowed to flourish. It's a limited palette of plants but it works beautifully to create a subtle, soft and cushioned experience as you move around the garden. The paving in my garden is currently being grown through by the thuggish *Crocosmia* that pops up all over the place. This pushes my little paving slabs up at jaunty and trip-inducing angles and looks really wrong as it grows through the cracks. I am going to tackle this, probably in the winter or next year, once I have found or saved up and bought some lovely reclaimed bricks and slabs to replace what's there. Adding a little geometry, and growing these softening plants in between the paving I lay, is a stroke of genius that I genuinely hadn't considered.

Amanda's plant choices are very similar to the ones I have gone for, though she's less focused on including useful plants than I am. She has again added extra formality, modernity and structure with cubes of box on the corner of each bed, but the essence of her planting is mixed ornamental grasses, mainly *Deschampsia* and *Calamagrostis* along with

Stipa gigantea, and limited flowers including *Verbena bonariensis*, which appeared one day of its own accord but looks lovely, *Thalictrum delavayi* and a magnificent *Persicaria* absolutely humming with bees and pollinating wasps. These combinations looked really beautiful. In the far corner she is redeveloping and was experimenting with different combinations including the addition of oranges to the purples, which looked really lovely.

BELOW RIGHT:
Deschampsia cespitosa with common hedge nettle – Stachys officinalis.
What a triumph – I love the combination of purple and ochre.

LEFT:
The persicaria mass complimenting the modern timber building

Instead of a hedge made of grasses she has a proper hedge, which for her is perfect and gives her the privacy she needs but for me would be overkill, removing my sun and blocking my neighbours too much.

In all it was really interesting to see how a designer has approached a project of her own on a scale very similar to mine. Her garden is 11x13m, and mine is 9x10m, so in scale and shape at least they are very comparable, even if hers is a little larger. She was in her garden for some years before she even started to plan it, so it makes sense that the design would be really strong. She said she packed far more plants into it than she would for one of her clients, which I was glad to hear as I have done exactly the same thing in my own.

Once I settle into my garden and get to know it better, I'm sure I'll start to feel comfortable with the idea of putting my own stamp on it rather than feeling the need to honour what is there already. This process will take time, however. I don't yet know where I will sit, for instance, as I have been so focused on plants and beds and greenhouses; another good reason to postpone work on the shelter and paving area until I know that's what I want it to remain. It might be that in time I decide to move the seating area somewhere else entirely.

At the moment I have planting around the edges of the garden, but my instinct is not usually to do that. I am not a huge fan of gardens with the traditional lawn flanked on all sides by beds. My beds are large and stick out into the lawn in places, but it's interesting that for my first ever garden, a space that's all mine and in which I can have total free rein, I have created a scheme which is so traditional. I imagine that once I get more confident with the idea of actually owning a garden and bond with the space more on my own terms, I will move away from the safe and traditional and push it a little more into my comfort zone. I love Mediterranean schemes, for example, but I haven't got faith that Mediterranean plants will survive in my garden. Perhaps after some experimenting with the plants I will learn exactly where the boundaries are in terms of what will survive here.

The point I am making is that no garden is ever finished. A year in a small garden is enough to begin to make your mark, if you try really hard. It's also no shame (in fact it might be very sensible) if after a year all you have done is observe and maintain what you have. Either way, it is just the beginning. Amanda's garden reminded me of a part of my own design aesthetic that I had forgotten in the pressure to try to create something cohesive. It reminded me that I have time to make mistakes, change my mind and work things out as they emerge. It reminded me to play and have fun. And that's always a nice lesson to take away from a garden.

6

Lawns

3 September

The grass seed heads are coming into their own — not in the garden I have to say, as they're too newly planted, but everywhere else, including the allotment. It is a tantalising vision of what's to come at home next year! I have been busy filming this year, but have seen some lovely grass-led planting schemes on my travels in the North and London. It's great to see. The weather has been quite warm, though still very wet. I have started trying to dry flowers before the end of the summer — on a rather fetching branch of witch hazel I hung in the winter — but finding dry mornings now that the dew has started and the rain continues, is a little challenging.

I keep seeing small-leaved plants around paving and wondering if it is something I should include in my own garden. Especially as the lawn is patchy along the trodden parts.

14 September

Everywhere I go, I see amazing paving, cossetted by moss and mind-your-own-business. In this damper climate I have tried to work out how to embrace the flora while remaining true to my aesthetic. I have made a good start on the garden and despite initially wanting to keep the lawn, I can see that with this amount of rainfall, the grass suffers. There are a lot of bare patches. I am finding these green, rustic pathways and patios really inspiring, and planting the seed of an idea to abandon my lawn and instead create a ramshackle, reclaimed path and patio with old bricks. I am back in my comfort zone here, creating permeable hard landscaping, but I think the garden will look much better for some additional structure. It won't be this year, but in time. I cut the lawn into a formal circle thinking that might give the structure it needs, but it doesn't exactly push the boat out. I'll mull it over.

23 September
The greenhouse jungle

It really is a jungle in the greenhouse now. It catches the best of the sun and I (and Rua) have taken to hanging out in there. It is warm and bountiful. The tomatoes are growing really well, though not quite turning red - fingers crossed soon - and the shrubs are settling in. Again, with that 'bricky' inspiration I keep seeing everywhere at the moment, I am thinking more and more of turning this greenhouse into more of a room, with plants of course. Maybe some old bricks on the floor, with a little table or a chair, and planting pockets around the outside for the shrubs. Pots can stand on the floor or the shelves. I think this would make a lovely place to be and grow. I have a peach and an apricot, so I think training them to grow as espaliers on each end, plus a few tomatoes, and shelves full of potted tender herbs and pelargoniums would make a completely incredible sitting area!

A municipal planting scheme I saw in a public space in London. This perfectly encapsulates the beauty of a mass of grass seed, used on a much bigger scale than I intend to in my garden. I hope, once things settle, it looks this good in my garden.

Lawns

Putting pen to paper and starting this chapter is difficult for me because there is so much I feel I want to say about (and to) the lawn.

The first is probably sorry. I have been one of the voices clamouring against this British garden staple for some years. The lawn has long occupied a position of huge importance in the garden, often being given pride of place as the central feature. And yet it is a monoculture, manicured and unnaturally kempt, and a very challenging place for wildlife to thrive. This point of view has grown in popularity recently, to the point where modern garden design has begun to vilify the lawn. This trend involves removing the lawn, but all too often it's replaced with slabs, plastic grass and concrete. A lawn may be a monoculture, but it has many beneficial attributes, like the ability to drain and protect against flash flooding and storm water, the ability to house soil-dwelling microbes, fungus and insect larvae, and the ability to breathe. It is also 100 per cent compostable. I added my voice to a call to consider the wildlife by being less reliant on lawns, and especially lawn chemicals, and instead found myself inadvertently part of a movement that made the situation for the wildlife in our gardens and the environment as a whole much more grave. And for that I am sorry.

This may be one of the first periods in history since the lawn's invention in the 1700s that it is not deemed particularly trendy. It's become such a ubiquitous part of our gardens that it may surprise you to hear that its conception in the English Landscape movement, developed by designers like William Kent, was an act of revolution. It was a totally unique concept: to curate a patch of grass that would previously have been grazed. The revolution was against the architectural garden; the kind we think about when we imagine a Tudor monarch strolling around their grounds – the knot gardens, parterres, arbours, mazes and hedges. The English Landscape garden is characterised by sweeping green views and parkland trees, with the pastoral landscape (or at least a sanitised version of it) stretching right from the door and out as far as the eye can see. Large lakes, ha-has (ditches designed to be invisible barriers keeping livestock away from the house) and, of course, lawns, were the cornerstones of these kinds of designs, which you can see in grand properties like Stowe, Chatsworth, Blenheim and Stourhead.

RIGHT:
The transition from grass into flower bed has always been something I have struggled with in terms of design. I love how it is shown here, where there is no edge, just short grass, then long grass.

Lawns, although they represented a rebellion, were not a grassroots one (if you'll forgive the pun). The intense non-mechanised upkeep of the lawn, using scythes and inordinate amounts of manpower, was hugely expensive. It was a luxury, as it meant less grass for the livestock, and therefore a feature exclusively found in the gardens of the super-wealthy elite. Lawns were a status symbol. It was not until a mechanised form of grass maintenance, the cylinder mower (still the preferred mower for a really top-notch lawn finish), was invented, that lawns became more commonplace. Though being able to dedicate such a large portion of the garden to an essentially useless space was still mainly the preserve of the wealthy. Less wealthy gardeners would generally have needed to utilise their limited space by growing food.

As lawns became slowly more attainable over the centuries, and food growing became less of a necessity, they grew in popularity to the point where they became an expected part of any garden. I don't think many of us questioned the lawn as a concept until relatively recently. Through the Cottage Garden movement, the Arts and Crafts movement, Modernist gardens, even in the famous and now much berated 1990s bamboo and decking era, the lawn was ever-present.

I have fond childhood memories of my mum's and my grandma's gardens, with lawn, small ponds and wildernesses, flanked by mixed borders of shrubs and flowers, as was the fashion at the time.

But that was before I was a gardener. Now, I find it a struggle to work with lawns in terms of design. The extreme artifice of a flat, green lawn, especially when it butts up against the dance of dangling and mingling flowers in a border, is jarring to me, whether it be hardened with stone or metal edges, or just a crisp, clipped grass edge.

I have to confess to finding the look of plants draping themselves on hard sandstone, or quarry tiles, or brick, much more pleasing to the eye than on to a deep verdant and vivid sward. My favourite and probably my signature style has become to replace a lawn with shingle and plant plants in that. Gravel can also breathe and drain in a very similar way to the lawn, and plants can self-seed and pop up through the gravel. This can also work with paving laid in a careful and concrete-free way. Allowing plants to seed themselves through

the surfaces requires editing rather than heavy hoeing and weeding, or relying on chemical herbicides mainly because gravel and shingle acts as a really good weed-supressing mulch. This shingle also reminds me of home, and the smooth rounded pebbles filled with volunteer plants like sea kale, fennel, viper's-bugloss and poppies that scatter themselves along the wide drifts of coastline under big skies.

The question is, why am I not planning on employing this gravelly style in the new garden? The answer is that there is something so lovely and simple about the space I have inherited. The soft lawn underfoot is so welcoming. And for the dog, a patch of grass for little zoomies feels like a kind thing to include. Also, a huge part of garden design is about being in keeping with the locale. And where I am, in soggy Dartmoor winters, the light-reflecting gravel will quickly turn green with algae and resemble not a glistening Mediterranean clifftop, but the base of a fish tank. So for now, the grass can stay.

The thought of lying of soft grass and looking up at the sky above my head in my very own garden, connecting directly with the earth beneath me and feeling safe, supported and home, feels right. There are also practical considerations – for example, taking delivery of tonne bags of pebbles would be a huge challenge in the little alleyway that you need to get through to access the garden. There are stones aplenty already in the garden, but they are the harsh, craggy, sharp rocks of the moor, not the smooth, rounded pebbles worn by millennia of tides and currents on the Kent coast of my childhood. These grey, rugged rocks look right in their setting, and I am sure that the smooth stones would look very wrong.

Lawns as habitat and wildflower meadow

As I mentioned, there is a lot more merit in a lawn than a patio, but there is yet more merit in a wildflower meadow. In fact grassland habitat is some of the most under threat in the UK and Europe, with around 97 per cent of wildflower habitat being lost in Britain, according to research from Kew Gardens. They are a very diverse habitat too, with nectar-rich plants often mingling with grasses or sedges and mosses, permanent ground cover for safe passage and habitat, and large areas of sunny, open ground, necessary for the survival of certain species, in particular for butterflies. As gardeners – especially those of us with larger gardens, or access to community gardens – we have the ability to add to a threatened habitat and provide safe refuge for species that find few homes elsewhere.

Just the other day I sat myself down in a wildflower meadow and drew a little sketch of the view, down the River Dart. After about 20 minutes of sitting there, to my right, immediately beside me but totally hidden from view, a field mouse started to squeak and chatter. It sounded like it was cross. Perhaps with me, or perhaps with another of its kind. Every few minutes, it would pipe up again and prattle away. If I looked very closely I could see the blades of grass shifting as the little mouse moved through the sward, but other than that, and its noise, which I wouldn't have heard if I had not been sitting so still, I would have had no idea that a mouse was there at all. This served as a lesson to me that just because you don't see something in the wild, it doesn't mean it isn't there, or isn't important.

Wildflower meadow is not a homogenous habitat, either. Meadows in different environments have different plant communities. Depending on where you are you may find various wetland meadow communities, open sunny meadow mixes, chalk meadows, upland meadows, lowland meadows, acid meadows, woodland meadows, meadows rich with grass, meadows rich with flowers, and a corresponding variety of species in each. Meadows themselves are characterised by very species-rich plant communities. The NVC (National Vegetation Classification) divides grassland habitats into ten broad groups. These are mesotrophic grassland, calcicolous grassland, calcifugous grassland and montane communities, aquatic communities, swamp and tall herb fens, salt marsh communities, shingle, strandline and sand-dune communities, maritime cliff communities and open habitats. So you can see that no matter what your garden faces in terms of its climate, there will be a kind of meadow that will thrive there.

There is usually one dominant species in any plant community, and generally in meadows it will be a grass that gives its type its namesake. But crucially, in a healthy meadow, a single quadrant should be home to numerous plant species, at different height levels, which come into their season at different times of the year to really maximise the usability for as wide a range of animals as possible. Each species will have different environmental benefits too, for example efficacy of nitrogen storage, ability to fix nitrogen, water uptake and the prevention of soil erosion, so as many species as possible is key.

There is a lot of work being done to try to repair the meadow habitats we have lost over recent centuries. I am a huge supporter of these efforts. Movements like the petitions to keep road verges unmown and active regeneration of meadowland by charities like Plantlife are making the picture more positive, bit by bit. But there is still a long hill to climb.

Creating a wildflower meadow

If you want to introduce or create a wildflower meadow, you can just stop mowing your grass, but you will find the meadow dominated by grass rather than flowers. To get varied flowers you need to reduce the fertility of the soil, as wildflowers like low fertility in general, and to weaken the vigour of grass species in order to open up patches of soil where flower seeds will have the chance to germinate. Often people plant something called yellow rattle, *Rhinanthus minor*, a plant that is hemiparasitic. That means that although it can photosynthesise it gets a lot of its nutrients from feeding off another plant. The yellow rattle feeds on grasses – members of the *Poaceae* family – and weakens them so flowers can germinate.

Resplendent grapes growing in a modest pot, up a wall

The really practical and productive structures here are designed to provide both design features and produce. Born out of necessity, executed with ingenuity.

Here, though, the addition of huge ponds in raised beds (something I am likely to mimic in front of my greenhouse in the future) and varied planting means that there is a different kind of edge and corridor habitat from your average railway track.

Overall I took away a feeling of real warmth from my trip to Bristol. It is a city I love. I have lived there on and off through my life and have always felt a real affinity with it. It houses vigour, excitement, unpredictability, fun, greenery, culture, art and an edge that I have always feared and respected in equal measure. Of course, like any city, it is hard to tame, and Bristol's energy makes this even more apparent. To be shown these spaces with such big-heartedness, invited to share the produce, muck in and help, and enjoy discussions about community, compost, plants (of course!) and so much more was wonderful. From Luke (an old friend) I expected nothing less, but from Sara, so respected in this field, it was especially lovely to be welcomed in with such generosity.

This project is living proof that gardening is about so much more than just aesthetic considerations and produce: it is integral to us as humans. We all come from nature, and are a part of nature. To have been separated from it can be very cruel. To enable that reconnection to happen is powerful and brave, challenging at times, and unequivocally, unquestionably necessary.

BELOW:
A beautiful marriage of form, function and habitat all in one insect-welcoming herb bed

RIGHT:
The joy of gardening and catching up with old friends

7 Planting

1 October
(Apple Day)

The last filming days with *Gardeners' World*. The sun actually shone for the filming this time, which made a nice change. Although I've really enjoyed trying out the main presenting role and it's forced me to get cracking on some garden jobs, I confess I am glad to have my garden back to myself. From now on I can see what happens and let it be for a while. There is no longer any pressure to progress it. Instead, I can take the time to observe and make the decisions slowly. I lost a friend the other week, a really close friend from school, so work on the garden has really slowed, as my weekends have been taken up with going home to see friends and grieve and also going to his memorial service back home, which was lovely. It feels apt to slow down now anyway, as autumn always brings a natural feeling of slowing down in me.

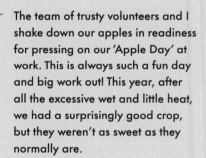

The team of trusty volunteers and I shake down our apples in readiness for pressing on our 'Apple Day' at work. This is always such a fun day and big work out! This year, after all the excessive wet and little heat, we had a surprisingly good crop, but they weren't as sweet as they normally are.

I'm no mycologist but I love mushrooms and fungi. I don't ever eat them, as I know enough to know that I don't know enough. But to observe them is always a fascination.

Some autumns make you fall in love with autumn. This year the colours here have been amazing. I have been walking in the woods all around my house and each day the colour seems to get better and better. The River Dart looks incredible too. Almost good enough to swim in, but after all the rain we have had it's a raging torrent. I spend a lot of my free time sitting in the garden and just contemplating it. I am also looking at lots of images, of other gardens and whatever inspiration I can get my hands on, to see where the next step of the garden might take me. I might extend the pond to make it more of a river that bisects the garden, or add more seating, or just leave it as it is for another year to assess its success before starting phase two — whatever that may look like. All the rain is at least giving me a chance to get some bits done in the house — finally! Autumn is always a time for nesting.

The principles of prairie planting

For me planting is everything. I have done some design work and built show gardens, but fundamentally I know I think like a gardener, not a designer.

I don't see in features and vistas and materials; it's thinking about the shape and positioning of the beds, and what plants will be in them, that excites and inspires me.

The one thing I have had clear in my mind for this new garden from the beginning is the planting scheme. It just sang out to me. I knew I wanted the whole space to envelop me in softness, and the lawn fading into the long grass, then grading into planted beds, heavy on grasses but still containing useful plants, was a concept that I envisaged as soon as I moved into the house.

Prairie planting is a style that has reigned supreme in herbaceous planting schemes for some years now. Although this style began to emerge just after 1900 in America, inspired by the work of architects like Frank Lloyd Wright, the modern iteration of it was really pioneered by Dutch garden designer Piet Oudolf in the 'New Perennial' style. This method of planting has since been exemplified by designers like Dan Pearson and growers like Neil Lucas, and is really well showcased in gardens such as Cambo Gardens in Fife, Scampston Hall in Yorkshire, and of course Sussex Prairie Garden.

I've long admired this style of planting, and am lucky to have had the chance to learn about it first-hand. My good friend Duncan Hall, who I trained with at Edinburgh, used to work at Cambo Gardens, and whenever I visited, I would admire the beds there. They are riotous and beautiful, but also totally self-supporting. They had a method of planting plants that would grow into a really good strong framework right next to plants that needed supporting and had a tendency to flop, to save themselves the work of staking. It was really effective and I used to quiz Duncan about it. I also spent some years working in a nursery and market garden that grew prairie plants (herbaceous perennials and grasses) for a big prairie nursery. I loved

RIGHT:
The generous swathes and textural finish of a prairie-style bed. My beds will have less structure and more chaos than this as there isn't room for this grand scale, but it's a style I certainly admire.

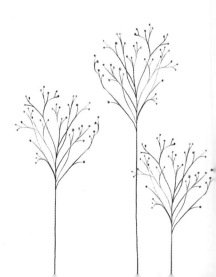

working there, and my then-boss and mentor Ian Harris taught me so much about how to grow these plants.

So what exactly is the prairie style? Generally speaking it is characterised by large drifts of planting, usually, though not always, dominated by grasses and North American herbacious perennials. Ribbons and swathes of single species slide off into the borders, usually in fairly informal lines. They cluster and flow around each other, catching the light and drawing your eye into the distance (see more inspiration on page 70.)

What I'm creating isn't completely faithful to the prairie style. For one thing my garden is far too small – I'll never have the wide, sweeping views across a linear landscape which are characteristic of the style in its most traditional iterations. But in recent years the prairie style has begun to evolve, and I'm taking inspiration from the ways in which others have played with it and adapted it.

BELOW:
A finished bed. I have pushed this style to its outer edges. Plants are dotted, not drifted, and it might look more meadow than prairie. In two years, once it settles and grows, I'll know if I've got it right!

healthy. Then plant them out, let them get through a winter and wait for flowers the following year. As a Mediterranean species it prefers a sunny, well drained spot.

Uses: clary sage is a commonly available essential oil with a lovely aroma, used in perfumes and cosmetics. It is also supposed to contain antibacterial compounds so is often used on the skin for healing, as well as for sprains and joint pain. The huge inflorescence is excellent for pollinators and a magnet for solitary bees. Flowers are also edible.

——

[13] SIBERIAN CHIVES *(Allium nutans)*
A chive-like clump-forming plant but with wider, strappy leaves and much larger flowers, which form later than traditional chives.

Cultivation: dying back in the winter, these perennials will need cutting back so that they can reshoot in the spring. Grow in a sunny spot with free draining soil.

Uses: there are some medicinal uses associated with members of the onion family (Allioideae) but they are more strongly attributed to onions and garlic themselves. Siberian chives are more commonly considered a culinary crop, being great used exactly like a chive; chopped and used as a garnish. The flowers are also really attractive to pollinators.

——

[14] TARRAGON *(Artemisia dracunculus)*
A highly aromatic herb native to warmer regions of Europe. It has fine stems with delicate leaves, and very occasionally yellow flowers – though generally it will not flower.

Cultivation: this tender herb needs protection from frost over the winter so dig it up and bring it indoors in the autumn. As it doesn't

generally flower and even when it does it doesn't tend to produce viable seed, division and by stem tip cuttings is the best way to propagate tarragon. Cuttings, like with many tender plants, are best taken at the end of the summer around August/September time.

Uses: used widely in cooking, adding a very distinctive flavour of anise to dishes. It can be used with vegetables or in salsa verde, but most traditionally is used with chicken or pork. Medicinally, it is said to be a digestive aid.

———

YACÓN *(Smallanthus sonchifolius)*
A South American member of the daisy family, with yellow flowers and huge, spade-shaped leaves which are something in between reniform and spatulate. The plants themselves can get up to two metres tall and have thick root tubers.

Cultivation: can be tender, so if in doubt, protect it in the winter, either by digging the tubers up and storing them in a cool, dark, dry place, or potted up in pots, not kept to wet. Or mulch the ground and leave them in the earth. I have always found they come back fairly well here in Devon, and also in Kent. In the north though, especially in regions that get very cold and very wet, they will be better off being lifted. Division of the tubers is very easy to propagate more plants.

Uses: this is a root vegetable as the tubers are edible. Raw they taste a little like apple, despite looking like potato, but are perfectly safe to eat. You can also cook them; roasting is the common method.

———

[15] SKIRRET *(Sium sisarum)*
A member of the carrot family, with small sprays of white flowers, neat compound leaves with opposite leaflets, and thick white roots.

Cultivation: this is a perennial plant, so needs cutting back each winter. If you are going to harvest it you can also grow it in a pot. Hardy, and fairly tolerant of most soils, this is a good general purpose plant.

Uses: this is a perennial parsnip replacement. It was once really popular and widely grown, but now much rarer. I have never eaten it but as I have now been growing it for some years, and bulking up my plants, it should be ready to harvest this winter.

———

[16] ALECOST *(Tanacetum balsamita)*
A very aromatic herbaceous perennial with rubbery, oval leaves which throw up tall stems and produce small yellow flowers. A close relative of tansy, the flowers are very similar.

Cultivation: this is a remarkably durable plant that copes well with sustained drought and also high water levels. That makes it perfect for gardens that are very wet in winter and dry in summer. Technically their leaves, both scented and waxy, with silver colouring, would mark them as a sun lover, but I have found them to be tolerant of many conditions, including salty atmospheres.

Uses: this is a traditional brewing herb. Many years ago hops, with their soporific effect, were ruled the only aromatics that could be used in brewing. Before that, though, there were many traditional brewing plants which were much more stimulating and probably made very interesting drinks.

———

[17] CHILEAN GUAVA *(Ugni molinae)*
A compact, evergreen shrub with small, dark, waxy leaves a little like a myrtle. It produces white flowers, followed by shiny, dark red berries in the late summer.

Cultivation: this needs sunlight but doesn't like to bake too hot. Being from Chile originally, it can cope with cold as long as it isn't cold and wet, but in a really hot, baking area it will need watering. It can be tender but I have kept it outside happily for years and only ever lost one, which suffered from extreme drought in a summer, followed by a very cold and wet winter. A lethal combination in this case.

Uses: the fruits are a really interesting flavour, like a mixture between a fruit and a bay leaf. I really like them though and with evergreen leaves, it's also really useful for winter structure.

———

MASHUA *(Tropaeolum tuberosum)*
A beautiful climber with peltate leaves, and an intricately lobed leaf margin that almost renders the leaves trifoliate. It has red tubular

flowers and nodules of root tubers.

Cultivation: this plant is not fully hardy, though it has got through the last few winters in Devon. Planting them nice and deep, or mulching them with compost or straw during the winter, should be enough. If your soil is very cold and very wet through the winter months, then the best thing is to lift them and store them for the winter in cool compost that isn't allowed to get too wet.

Uses: mashua is a root vegetable from South America, particularly the Andes. It is a really close relative of common nasturtium but a perennial form. Although the leaves and flowers (if it forms them, which it only does in a very good year) are edible, just like nasturtium, it is really grown for its edible tubers, which taste a little like wasabi and can be used instead of water chestnuts in a stir-fry.

Low-level planting

SELF-HEAL *(Prunella vulgaris)*
A ground cover wildflower with little spikes of purple/blue flowers that appear in the summer.

Cultivation: this can grow in a really varied range of places. It often occurs in lawns so can compete for space very well, in both full sunshine and in deep shade. It can be a really useful ground cover in spots where you struggle to establish strong plants.

Uses: as the name suggests this is a medicinal herb. It has been used to treat coughs and dizziness, as well as skin complaints. Other names include heal-all, woundwort, carpenter's herb and heart-of-the-earth. It is an ingredient in many herbal teas and the young foliage is edible. The blue flowers are fantastic for pollinators.

---

[18] ROMAN CHAMOMILE
(Chamaemelum nobile)
Lawn chamomile is another name for this plant. Tiny spreading leaves hug the ground releasing gentle scent when they're walked on and bearing small white daisy flowers with skirt-like petals and a yellow centre.

Cultivation: full sun and a fairly free draining soil. Although this is called lawn chamomile, it doesn't like to be walked on as much as grass so it's best to avoid it in heavy footfall areas. It can also cope with more shade than it says on the tin, so it's a fairly resilient plant.

Uses: traditionally the flowers of this plant are dried and used medicinally for teas that help with insomnia, but it's also used for many cosmetics, including for hair and skin care.

have softened the soil before you dig your plants up, and to water in your newly divided plants once they go back into the ground.

✴ Tips for success

Plants generally don't like having their roots messed around with too much. If you are going to cause root damage and disturbance, then it's always a good idea to reduce stress on the parts of the plant that are above the ground by cutting back the growth, by up to about half, and certainly by removing the flowers and seeds that might be trying to form, so the plant can put all its energy into producing new roots. Keep newly planted plants well watered.

Cuttings

Producing cuttings is pure magic. Imagine snipping off a finger and sticking it in the ground, and then watching a whole new you, genetically identical, grow. That's what happens when we take cuttings. It really is amazing.

THE PROCESS

[1] Use a non-flowering stem from the plant. This can be a long stem or just the tip. Cut it off just above a convenient bud (otherwise known as a node). Keep it moist and fresh while you're gathering all your cutting material (best done in the early morning, when the plants are still fresh from the cool night air) or get them into the soil as quickly as you possibly can. You can put them into a sealed plastic bag for freshness. Prepare some containers with peat-free seed and cutting compost and have them at the ready.

[2] Now create your cutting. Remove all the lower leaves from the stem, leaving only the top pair. You can pinch the very tip out at this stage to create a bushier plant but it isn't necessary and can be the source of introduced infection.

[3] Once you have essentially a stick, with just two leaves on the top, make a hole the right length with a dibber (long enough so that the whole stem fits in, with just the top leaves emerging from the compost and the base hitting the bottom of the hole).

[4] Cut the bottom off the stem, to just below a node, and put your cutting in. Some people like to do this around the edge of the pots as the heat promotes rapid root growth and encourages roots branching, and others like to put the cuttings a little way from the edge so that roots can develop the whole way around the plant rather than just on one side. You can find whatever way suits you.

[5] Firm the soil in around them and give them a water at the base. Keep the compost damp but not too wet until you can see roots have formed through the holes in the base of the pot. The time this takes will, of course, vary depending on species and conditions.

WHEN TO DO IT

Generally this will be in spring or summer, well before flowering, though of course depending on the type of cutting you take you might want to do it in autumn or winter. Soft wood cuttings are taken in spring. Semi-ripe cuttings are in mid or late summer, and tender plants are best done in late summer too. Hard wood cuttings are taken in winter, and root cuttings (simply cutting up roots and placing them in or on soil) are taken in autumn or winter. You will get to learn this as you get to know your plants.

✳ Tips for success

Introducing fungus to a cutting is a sure-fire way to kill it. Make sure you work with clean tools and in fairly sanitised conditions. Also use fresh compost, not reused compost. You can use hormone rooting powder to keep fungus to a minimum too.

The absolute crucial thing to get right is the moisture balance. Without roots, a plant is liable to lose excessive moisture through the leaves (that's why you've removed most of them) without being able to take it up very efficiently. But you also mustn't let the tips get too damp, because fungus thrives in damp conditions. Make sure the compost is moist, but the atmosphere is not too wet.

Seed sowing

It never ceases to amaze me that a tiny acorn can (literally) grow a mighty oak. That a kale seed is no bigger than a flea and yet it produces a huge, nourishing vegetable. That in a single season, a sunflower seed can dwarf a bungalow, and that from a single pumpkin seed, your whole garden can be taken over with enormous, orange, plump pumpkins.

THE PROCESS – THIS IS REALLY SIMPLE.

[1] Choose your seeds, fill a tray with fresh seed and cutting compost (peat free), firm it down, and place your seed in or on the compost. The bigger the seed, the deeper it needs to be planted; generally it's around three times the depth of the seed, though this varies, with some seeds needing light and others complete dark.

[2] Then sprinkle over a little extra compost, LABEL THE TRAY and place the whole tray into a water bath until it is completely soaked.

[3] Take it out of the water and keep it warm and away from rats and mice until the second set of leaves has grown (the first set doesn't necessarily mean the seed is strongly established, as they are already waiting inside the seed case).

[4] Once the second set of leaves has grown, gently and carefully remove the seedlings and put them into their own pot until they are big enough to go out into the garden. This is a generic seed story. Some need to go through a cold period called stratification before they will germinate. Some need to be soaked in water for 24 hours. Some need to be roughed up or cut, known as scarification, before they can germinate. Generally a good seed packet will give you really clear instructions on the back. Just follow those if in doubt.

WHEN TO DO IT

In most cases the timing is fairly critical, especially with vegetables. Again the seed packets will tell you exactly when to sow your seeds, but as a general rule you can't go wrong with spring. There are a few exceptions to the rule but if you get something growing once the weather is consistently warm, then you will give your seedlings a whole growing season to get nice and big and healthy.

✳ Tips for success

Never let your seeds dry out once they are sown. The initial soaking of the seeds (called imbibition) breaks their dormancy and gets all the signals going to initiate growth. If at this stage they dry out then those signals (now spent) get interrupted and will never restart. So keep them permanently moist but not really wet. Once leaves appear you can gauge the moisture levels by looking at the leaves.

8

The
Allotment

November

Autumn colour has come to the garden! The Morello cherry and the ginkgo look incredible, both are butter yellow. It makes me wonder if there might be room for another small tree — something pink, orange or even red in the autumn. I went for a walk today and saw a lovely *Viburnum × bodnantense* just coming into bloom. I wonder if that might be something to consider. Though the sun has now completely gone from the garden, so perhaps reserving the crowning glories of the garden for the summer months when the sun shines bright and full into the space is a better idea. The grape (which sadly dropped the last of its fruit in the recent cold snap) also has stunning autumn colour, especially with the rose hips. I love that gnarled, hag-like look of autumn. It is so reminiscent of children's stories by the fireside. Of cold days and cosy evenings by the woodburner, that's what autumn reminds me of. All the russet and the golden browns of the garden really evoke that.

A magnificent beech tree showing its finery of gold, russet and green. One of my favourite autumn trees.

Mashua leaves still hanging on in this mild autumn we've been having. The tubers, which are the bit you eat, should be fine in a little frost. However, as soon as it turns cold, these leaves will disappear.

Enjoying the greenhouse. There was a time when I wondered if putting the greenhouse in the sunniest corner of the garden had been a mistake — where was I supposed to sunbathe? Slathered in factor 50 of course! — but it has really come into its own. When nothing else in the garden has sun and warmth, the greenhouse does. It's a little microclimate. All the more reason to convert it into a little writing room. As I write this, I think how lovely it would be to have a little table in the sunshine, a cup of coffee beside me, and write in the open(ish) air. There is a small leak that drips through the old door on the roof and leaves dampness on the floor, and drought on the beds. I might shift the two areas around, or try to repair the leak, as the plants look parched and the standing area is a little boggy. I harvested and cut down all my tomatoes (a small bowlful), peppers and chillies the other day. So the jungle is gone, but the sun is let in with renewed vigour!

My allotment gardening principles

I have been a keen allotment grower for as long as I have been able. When I was a child, my newly single mum took on a plot at our local allotment, about a half-hour walk from our house.

It was overgrown and covered in junk: old carpet, rubber, wire, pallets, brambles everywhere. My two sisters and I were less than helpful there. My good friend's parents had another plot, so I remember lots of rioting and running around, and absolutely no attempt to help my mum from any of us.

Like many of us allotment growers, my mum found it a big time commitment while also trying to hold down a job and raise three challenging children, but my mum is amazing at seeing the long game. Bit by bit she cleared the whole plot of all of its rubbish. It took her a year to get through it, but she managed. Sadly, though, because she had spent the year clearing it and not growing on it, she was asked to vacate by the allotment association; an injustice that I still find tragic. I suspect that in reality a part of her felt relieved to have this extra responsibility removed from her shoulders, but I do remember her feeling pretty aggrieved at the situation. This experience helped shape my feelings that access to land should be for all – even, or perhaps especially, overworked and time-poor single parents like my mum, who may not work fanatically or produce award-winning veg, but need a little place to escape to.

I have very fond memories of playing there, and gained a sense that a community growing space, a shared endeavour, was something I wanted to be a part of.

During my time in Edinburgh I worked in community gardens and further explored this idea of working as a collective to grow food, but it wasn't until I first moved to Devon that I felt in any way settled enough to add my name to a long waiting list and get an allotment of my own. In the nearly six year wait that followed, I moved around a lot – to Bristol, then Devon, then back to Kent with my mum, where a plot was immediately available in the small village she now lives in.

After that I moved to Folkestone, from where I still kept up that allotment through the pandemic, and finally back to Devon.

By this time, I was at the top of the waiting list for an allotment. I shared a plot for a time with my friend Tracy, but then when she got her own plot, I took on ownership myself. It is a much smaller and more temperate plot than the Kent one, which lay in the middle of a desolate marsh. This one is silty, sheltered, surrounded by a stream, not baked by full sun but fairly shady, with sun from about 2pm until sunset (a blessing as it saves on watering, which has to be done with a watering can) and is my happy place.

Each allotment site has its own rules that plot holders must abide by. My Kent allotment allowed sheds, glass and hosepipes, none of which are allowed here in Devon, but it also was more draconian about what you could grow, with no more than 20 per cent being allowed for flowers. (I had a ready counter-argument about what constitutes a flower – after all, without its flowers we wouldn't have tomatoes, aubergines, beans, courgettes, squashes, cucumbers or any other fruiting plant . . . but luckily, despite a few murmurings about how many cut flowers I was growing, I never had to present this case in front of the committee). The Kent allotment also had a more old-fashioned view about biodiversity. I was not allowed even a small pond for health and safety reasons, and weeds or wildflowers were actively discouraged. The plot in Devon, on the other hand, is openly welcoming to permaculture and no-dig principles, as well as to creating a diverse habitat.

My new plot's miniscule size means that I was easily able to get on top of it – weed it, cultivate it, mulch it and replant it – in a single day. But it also made designing it a challenge. I knew it was too small to fit a shed, which I had found to be such a haven and place of restful solitude on the Kent allotment, so the space was exclusively for growing.

I am completely chemical-free when I grow. So I feed the allotment plants with comfrey, nettle, and seaweed feed, or with a mulch of manure, which is provided on the plot for a small donation. I try to disturb the soil and soil microbes as little as possible by minimising how much digging and walking on the soil I do. And I try to provide as much varied habitat and wildlife-friendly planting as I can. I do get pheasants, rabbits, pigeons and many insects visiting the plot but I do not fence it. I let animals come and share my produce. In the hungry gap animals are hungry too.

RIGHT:
Some would find the chaos of my allotment messy, but I love it. Veg are hidden amongst herbs, flowers and perennials, so it's a real adventure and feels very natural – almost like foraging.

The design

The whole plot is rectangular, and about 10x3m. I created a simple design that maximises beds and minimises paths. The single path bisects the plot in a continuous zigzag, creating a series of triangles that you move past as you walk the length of the plot. The zigzag goes right to the edge of the plot, so that you can enter and exit at any point without having to weave your way up and down the whole plot each time you want to get to the other end. There are straight paths down the two sides that separate my plot from my neighbours'. Around the far bottom edge and up one side, in an L-shape, I have erected chestnut posts that act as a fence, up which I grow espalier fruit, hops, grapes and some climbing fruit like wineberries and loganberries.

Each triangle has an allotted function. When you first approach the plot from the main pathway, you come to the top two triangle beds. One is the cut flower bed, made up of a core of herbaceous perennials, which I interplant with annuals each spring. The next is a herb and perennial vegetable bed. Though it has yielded some really nice crops over the years, this part of the allotment now needs a bit of a rethink and a refresh; some things have taken over and others been lost, so I will spend the autumn weeding, thinning and planting some fresh plants. The next triangle you come to is the largest one, the annual veg triangle, which is sunny and open. Finally, you end at the soft fruit triangle, at the corner of which is a little bench where I can sit and munch and watch the sun go down.

Cut flower growing

As I have explained, ornamentals grown purely for the sake of ornament are of not much interest to me. Plants that are botanically interesting, have a compelling story or history, or have some use, are what really get me excited. So cut flowers might seem an odd thing to prioritise. But about seven years ago I had a lovely experience of picking them in a field at a garden I used to work in down here in Devon, and that converted me. Walking through a baking hot field, surrounded by flowers as far as the eye can see, and picking yourself a little bunch to take home with you is a beautiful experience, both decadent and wholesome at the same time.

My cut flowers, however, also serve as companion plants and pollinator-friendly additions that will increase biodiversity and create a thriving and productive plot that welcomes all creatures. As such I have seedheads in the form of three *Calamagrostis brachytricha* and *Echinacea purpurea* as well as lots of pollinator-friendly plants that progress through the year a little like this:

RIGHT:
A bunch of spring/early summer flowers from the plot. *Angelica* seed heads with *Nepeta*, *Knautia* and *Digitalis*.

SPRING
Bulbs including white scented daffodils, Alliums, tulips and Camassia, Siberian iris (*Iris sibirica*), and forget-me-nots that spring up everywhere.

SUMMER
Lychnis coronaria, *Geranium*, *Tulbaghia*, *Perovskia*, *Nepeta*, *Echinacea*, *Helianthemum*, *Gypsophila*, *Scabiosa*, *Knautia macedonica*, *Anchusa* 'Loddon Royalist', *Salvia nemorosa*, *Cephalaria gigantea*, a perennial *Helianthus* and tansy, which I use for drying. I then add annuals and biennials like *Ammi majus*, *Helianthus annuus* ('Lemon Queen' and 'Valentine' are my favourites as well as 'African Queen'), *Cosmos sulphureus* and *bipinnatus*, *Cerinthe major*, *Coreopsis tinctoria*, sweet peas, *Tithonia*, *Angelica gigas*, *Digitalis*, *Borago officinalis* seeds itself all over, and I grow *Xerochrysum* for drying and whatever else I manage to find. I don't currently grow *Dahlia* as I trained in a garden that held the national collection of dark-leaved *Dahlia* and confess to getting a little sick of them. They aren't flowers I naturally love, except for the species ones, which are really beautiful. The overbred and bawdy ones aren't my cup of tea, but as I grow them now in a cut flower garden at work, I see their merit. They produce and produce and produce and they last well in a vase. So I am considering a foray into *Dahlia* cultivation. Watch this space.

AUTUMN
The grass seedheads really come into their own here. The *Calamagrostis brachytricha* has plumes of large purple seedheads that dry to the colour of straw. I pick and dry some, which last all through the winter and beyond, but I also leave some on the plant to catch the winter light. I intend to find space to also add some *Rudbeckia* at this time of year, which I love, especially with the *Verbena bonariensis* that seeds itself through the whole plot.

WINTER
Winter is not a great time for a cut flower garden, but it is the perfect time to continue admiring the seedheads and also to buy and plant more spring bulbs for next year, as you can never have too many. Despite being made to plant 50,000 with four other people during my first freezing winter as a gardener, aged 20, planting spring bulbs remains one of my favourite things to do. It's like burying treasure.

Herb growing

As you might imagine, growing herbs is a passion of mine. I love their function and I love their form. I love their scents, their flowers – generally high in pollen and valuable to the pollinators – and I love their secret stories and histories. I love what they represent about our own history, too, and our lost skills in the arts of healing ourselves, feeding ourselves and being at one with the plants around us. The more I learn about herbs, the more I find myself drawn to not only the beautiful and functional Mediterranean kinds that we're all fairly familiar with, but also the wild native herbs which we would once have relied upon but which are less popular and well documented nowadays.

To some extent this interest in native herbs has developed out of necessity, as I struggle to grow Mediterranean herbs in the Devon climate – on my allotment they may last a year, sometimes two, but they usually eventually rot and die. (My rosemary is the exception: it has grown into a large and really strong specimen, which has even made a full recovery from a devastating attack of rosemary beetle.) But I'm also deeply interested in the history of this lost herbal knowledge, which seems indicative of a more general and pernicious separation between society and nature that characterises our modern world. Herbs like *Achillea* or plantain have such interesting stories to tell about how humans and plants may have enjoyed a more symbiotic relationship in the past, and I love trying to bring this relationship back to life, even in small ways.

For this reason, and for the sake of biodiversity, I let some weeds stay on my allotment. Dandelion, with its long taproot capable of bringing up good nutrients from deep in the soil, capacity for carbon storage, soil improvement even in wastelands and through concrete, is also a powerful medicine used in detoxifying the liver, purifying the kidneys and helping with digestion. You can eat the leaves as well as the root. And yet we malign and vilify it as a weed. As a very wise and knowledgeable woman I know said to me just the other day, 'this native medicinal herb is the pin-up for weed killer. Look in your local garden centre and you will find that many of the herbicides will feature a dandelion on the packaging.' She was right.

And while I do grow herbs for their medicinal properties, mostly I grow them for culinary purposes. I relish being able to add my own fresh herbs to my cooking. I will now keep the tropical ones like lemongrass, ginger and Vietnamese coriander in my greenhouse

Russian tarragon harvest. Not quite the pinch of flavour of the French, but fresh herbs always taste so good.

at home. I also tend to grow coriander from seed as it is another favourite. In the herb garden I have Siberian chives, marjoram and oregano, *Achillea*, chives, valerian, lovage, marsh mallow, angelica, Sweet Sicily, celery leaf, parsley, chervil, caraway, chamomile, feverfew, mint, and a favourite of mine, winter savoury – better than thyme, which doesn't always survive very well, but with a similar flavour. This is a dainty little plant with small white flowers. I also grow a lot of tarragon, as this is a herb I love, though it needs to be dug up and brought in for the winter, being not remotely hardy.

Perennial veg growing

Here's what I grow in this part of the allotment:

PERENNIAL KALE

My favourite. I have one called Keeper and it's marvellous. It produces leave all year so I can harvest kale whenever I want. If it flowers, which it did this year, you can still cut from it. The leaves look rubbery but they are just as good in flavour and when cooked, in texture, as annual kale. Propagate it by chopping off a bit and sticking it in the ground. Et voilà!

RHUBARB

A stalwart of the allotment and of perennial veg. I love this plant with its delicious stems and generous leaves. To grow simply mulch it with manure each year. Some years rest it if it's looking like it's weakening. You can force the stems in spring but I never bother. More light means a healthier plant so I leave it in the open.

ASPARAGUS

Another classic perennial veg. This grows wild where I grew up but here in the south west I need to cultivate it. I planted mine two years ago so I can't harvest it until next year (fingers crossed, as it isn't looking too healthy this year). It is said that they don't like competition but back home they grow around the base of apple trees in the orchards so I can't see that this is always true. What they don't like is to sit in water, so the allotment might be too wet in the winter.

GOOD-KING-HENRY

A spinach alternative that was very popular at one time. The leaves are really tasty and it turns into a lovely little clump of green once it settles in.

HABLITZIA TAMNOIDES

Not a very good grower for me. Another spinach alternative, this is a climber, and it can get really vigorous if it's happy. I've had mine in for three years and it has done very little. It's still there but only a few inches tall. I think it might be time to replace it.

***BETA VULGARIS* (SEA BEET)**

A leafy vegetable closely related to chard and used as an alternative, which produces a large, beautiful flower spike, then turning to seedhead, which seeds itself around the place. This is a lovely and statuesque plant.

CLOCKWISE FROM TOP LEFT:
Perennial kale 'keeper', rhubarb, hopniss and asparagus

APIOS AMERICANA

A lovely North American root crop that tastes like potato. It's a member of the pea family so the crop is actually the nitrogen-fixing nodules on the roots. This is not hardy so I bring it in and keep the tubers I don't harvest in cool, slightly moist but frost-free compost for the winter.

HUMULUS LUPULUS (HOP)

Although I grow this as a climber around the edges of the whole plot, so that I can dry the cones and use them in sleepy pillows, the method of growing these plants involves training just two or three stems that will grow up from the base during the year. The rest of the shoots that come from the ground each year make a really good vegetable. Snip them off when they are about 15cm long, and they make a great alternative to asparagus.

ZINGIBER MIOGA (JAPANESE GINGER)

This is a fairly hardy plant that has made it through two cold winters on the allotment without being moved. Although it produces lovely healthy leaves, it is the flowers that appear right at the base that you eat. They have a lovely flavour, funnily enough, rather like ginger!

I am also growing mashua, yacón and skirret, as described in chapter seven – see pages 203-4 for more information.

BELOW:
Hop cones drying and generous leaves of the yacón

Annual veg growing

This is a really lovely but very intensive part of growing on an allotment. There is always more that you can be getting on with in annual vegetable production. Sowing generally starts around April and continues in successions through until October, though the last period of intensive sowing in our temperate climate is generally around August. The autumn sowings are for things like sweet peas and broad beans if you want to get ahead for next spring. Something that might help reduce your workload is growing into modules rather than seed trays. This removes the stage called 'pricking out' where you carefully separate the seedlings into their own pot. Sowing direct into modules means you can keep seedlings for much longer in their pots, grow them big and strong and then plant them out directly. You could even use things like old toilet rolls for this, then plant them out still in their pot or roll.

The main benefit of this method is that it saves you a huge amount of time, as pricking out is a really labour-intensive process, but also that you won't find yourself running out of space so quickly. In a small garden or allotment, or if, like me for many years, you're restricted to windowsill propagation, this is what seed sowing tends to look like: sow all your seeds in spring and fill every available windowsill with seed trays. All fine so far. Then, two or three weeks later, start pricking out all of your seedlings and find that where you were nicely full before, now you simply have no room left for any of your little seedlings, let alone to start sowing the next succession. The result is that you can soon start to feel overwhelmed and overrun by plants.

Modular growing means you know exactly how much space you have because seedlings go straight from the windowsill to harden off, then get planted in their modules in the ground. How many seeds you grow per module will vary depending on what you're growing. Kale, bulb fennel, lettuce and pak choi will prefer to be sown one seed per module, whereas beetroot, salad leaves, spring onions, celery, parsley, coriander and chard can be sown in groups. This is called multi-sowing. Root vegetables which don't like their roots to be disturbed, like parsnips, beetroot and carrots, can also really benefit from this method. For bigger seeds like cucumber, squash, peas and beans, small pots might be better than modules.

Basic seed sowing schedule for vegetables

I tend to grow a mix of vegetables, but there are a few staples that I would not be without. They include courgettes, squashes (which climb up the boundary fence if I can get them to), bulb fennel, chard, climbing and dwarf beans, and beetroot, I sometimes grow carrot and parsnip as I love them, though they take up a lot of space and I find germinating them challenging. Soaking them can help. Some years I grow potatoes and tomatoes, though I tend to grow tomatoes in the house as well in case we have a bad blight year. (Blight is a fungus that affects tomatoes and potatoes.) I used to grow annual kale and cabbage, but now I have the perennial kale I no longer do. I do still sometimes grow purple sprouting broccoli and sprouts.

[1] CHARD & PERPETUAL SPINACH
Sow March–June and August (for a winter, indoor crop) in modules with three to four seeds per module.

SPINACH
Sow March–May and August (for indoor winter crop) in modules of up to three seeds.

KALE & BRASSICAS
Sow February–June and August (for indoor kale and early outdoor brassicas next spring) in deep modules with one seed per module.

BEETS
Sow once the ground is warm – April and May for two successions in modules of three to four seeds, or direct into the soil. Thin as you harvest so the ones left will get big and juicy.

CELERY
Sow February–April, keep very well watered throughout the growing season. Sow in modules of up to four seeds per module.

FENNEL BULB
Sow April or when the soil warms up. One seed per module.

SPRING ONION
Sow March–August for lots of successions. Thin them if you want to bulk up a few onions. Sow up to ten per module.

LEEK
Sow early leeks as soon as it's warm (March) and later leeks from April to May. Sow in a big tray and plant out once they're the thickness of a pencil. Bury the whole stem underground when you plant it for nice, juicy leeks.

ONION
Sow early, around February, for a nice long season and big onions.

CARROT
Sow direct into nice, friable, deep soil or a deep container between April and the end of June.

PARSNIP
Either sow direct into the soil or (as I was advised when I was struggling with germination) allow them to start germinating on a wet tissue, then plant them once germination begins into compost-filled loo rolls, and plant them out in their pots when big enough. Put in one seed per loo roll. Sow outdoors from April to June; you can start a little earlier for the indoor tissue method.

CELERIAC
This plant need a long maturing season, so start them early indoors, around February, then harden them off and plant them out in April. Sow one seed per module.

[2] FRENCH BEANS (DWARF & CLIMBING)
Sow these once the weather is reliably warm. You can sow them direct into the ground but I prefer to sow them from April to May into small pots, two seeds per pot.

RUNNER BEANS
Exactly the same method as the French beans. With both of these, and peas, protect them from rats and rodents if you know you have them on the allotment.

[3] SALADS INCLUDING LETTUCE, MUSTARD, ROCKET, LANDCRESS
These are quick crops that can have multiple successions all through the year. Sow February (indoors) to July. If you want a winter crop growing under cover, sow it around August. Lettuce, one seed per module, the rest three to four.

PEAS

Early sowings work best. Sow March to early April, two seeds per pot or module. Remember to plant them in among pea sticks for them to climb or else they become a tangled mess.

BROAD BEAN

Sow in either autumn (October) or early spring (March) either in small pots or modules. One seed per module. You will be harvesting them at around the same time, no matter when they were sown.

CHICORY & ENDIVE

Cool temperature crops that taste too bitter in the height of summer. Best eaten in autumn, winter or early spring and good hungry gap crops. Sow February to June, one seed per module, but allow plenty of time for them to grow before you pick them.

PARSLEY

Sow March to May. I love growing parsley and sometimes it can almost become perennial and grow again even after it has flowered. Flat leaf parsley is easier to grow but curly leaf has a slightly better flavour. Three to four seeds per module.

CORIANDER

Easy to germinate even when the weather isn't warm. Sow in successions from February to October, but for late sowings protect from frost or eat as microgreens. Once it flowers, either eat or save the seeds. They are delicious when still green. Three to four seeds per module.

DILL

Sow March to June in successions. This crop tends to flower (bolt) really easily, so for lots of the delicious foliage, do many successions and multi-sow. Three seeds per module.

BASIL

Sow March to April, three to four seeds per module, or direct into a pot that can live on the windowsill. They do grow best indoors, in a greenhouse or polytunnel, or on a windowsill, but will grow well outside in a good summer.

[4] COURGETTE

These plants and other members of the cucurbit group grow best when the temperatures are warm. Sow April to May, one succession per year, one seed per pot, into small pots. Don't overdo it as these will produce an awful lot of fruits.

SQUASH

Sow mid-April, one seed per pot. You can let these wonderful plants climb to save space. Once you have harvested them, if you know you are rodent-free, and have a warm space under glass, cure them in a greenhouse for two weeks to toughen the skins, before storing them for the winter.

CUCUMBER

Sow March to April, one seed per small pot. These grow best indoors but you can also grow them outside. Although they like warmth, they don't do too well where it's very, very hot so a greenhouse that's not in full sun, or a very sheltered garden, would both do perfectly. They are climbers so don't take up much space.

SWEETCORN

Sow around May. They grow quickly. In a warm area you could get them started in April. Sow two per small pot, and plant the strongest seedlings in a warm, not too dry, and not too windy spot. The roots are very shallow so they can dry out quickly. Mulch them if you are worried.

[5] TOMATOES

These like a long growing season to develop fruits, so you can start them really early, but I find February or March the perfect time to get them started. Sow one seed per module. You can get bush varieties and cordon varieties (which means just one stem grows up a string) – either works fine, but just make sure you know what you have so you can plant them in the right place. Bush tomatoes can be grown in pots. Avoid grow bags as they are really not the best environment. A large pot will be much better.

PEPPERS

Another plant that has a long development season. Start these off in the warm (house or greenhouse on a heat mat) in January. One seed per module or small pot.

CHILLI

Exactly as pepper. Start them off on heat in January for a good crop. They both grow best indoors, but you can still get a decent crop outside. In a hot, dry year, they will be much spicier so be aware of that when choosing your variety.

AUBERGINE

Also needs a long growing season and warmth. They will grow best in the greenhouse or polytunnel. Sow seeds on heat and under protection from January to April. The lovely thing about growing these from seed is that there is a huge range of colours that look very beautiful. I have recently discovered grafted ones, and though they are more expensive, they are much higher yield.

Soft fruit growing

LEFT:

My lakemont grapes, carted from Kent to here, are finally fruiting for the first time. They were delicious. In order to get them to ripen I thinned the bunches. Ensuring there are one or two bunches per branch, I removed the smallest grapes on the bunch.

This is one of my favourite things to do. A little like perennial vegetables, soft fruit is so easy. You don't need to sow it each year, or water it within an inch of its life. The only thing you really need to do is cut it back in the autumn, or prune it, perhaps give it a little helping of manure around the base over the winter, and then (if you feel disinclined to 'share' all your berries with the pigeons) net it. I never do net it, so I hardly get any fruit, but the bits I do get are so delicious that I don't mind sharing. Feeding the wildlife is half of the reason I garden, so I am sanguine about feathered thieves. One thing I will say about that, though, is if you aren't going to be there often, then you should probably net, with eco-friendly netting so that small birds, reptiles, big bees and mice don't get tangled in the netting. And if you see something ripe, take it there and then, because next time it will be gone!

The fruits I grow are:

AUTUMN RASPBERRY
I don't bother with the summer raspberry, which fruits on its second year, because I have so many autumn raspberries and they are an extraordinarily delicious variety. (I have no idea what the variety is because they came with the plot.) This plant will produce and produce and produce from August right through until November. I love it, despite it being the worst weed on the plot and popping up absolutely everywhere! The more you pick the more fruit it makes.

GRAPES 'LAKEMONT'
Which are tied into the fence around the edge and has fruit for the first time this year. Prune this back in December or January when the plant is completely dormant. You can cut off the long green tendrils (without ever going into brown wood) in high summer. And thin the fruits so that they all ripen.

BLACKCURRANTS
My favourite fruit. I love their flavour and they're so hard to come by in the supermarket.

JOSTABERRY
A cross between blackcurrant, North American gooseberry and European gooseberry, they are meant to be really good but into year three mine still hasn't fruited so the jury is still out for me.

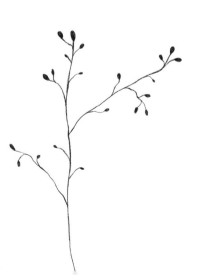

REDCURRANT

A really useful fruit. Not as delicious as blackcurrants but great in jams.

LOGANBERRY

A delicious cross between a blackberry and a raspberry. I love this plant. It climbs like a blackberry, so I tie it into the fence and train in new stems each year, which keeps it in check and keeps it producing loads of delicious berries. I have also added a tayberry, which is a very similar cross, but it has not fruited yet either so I am unable to compare them.

JAPANESE WINEBERRY

An interesting fruit. I cannot think of a more opulent and beautiful fruiting plant. It has red, spiky stems and green leaves, with fruits that glow like rubies. The only problem is that though it tastes alright, it doesn't have the complex flavour of the other berries. In that respect it is a little lacking. But apparently it makes wonderful jam. I had a bumper crop of them this year, but the pigeons got there first.

STRAWBERRIES

I have to mention these even though I never EVER get any. I have grown them on the ground. One day if I think of it when I'm there or if I find the time, I might pot up some runners into hanging baskets and hang them from the wall. As it is my invisible mouse friend eats them all before I get a look in.

RIGHT:
Japanese wineberry with glorious, fuzzy red stems

BELOW:
Strawberries growing on the ground among the herbs and perennial vegetables

The Next Year in my Small Garden

The first year in my first house has ended. The garden has begun to grow. Seeds planted, radical emerging and the beginnings of an idea beginning to take shape. The world will change, I will change and my space will grow and change with me. But there have been some interesting lessons, even in this first season.

I suppose, this year in my small garden has made me examine all the reasons why and how I garden. Why grow something if I don't get to eat it? Because I feel I am making a contribution to a world that I can't necessarily see, but I know and trust to be out there. As a gardener you are so intrinsically connected to nature, but in a strangely disengaged way. I see a tree and sometimes I forget to admire its beauty, or smell its resin, or count how many birds are currently on it. Instead I think I need to remove a branch or two, or that it's encroaching on the path.

It's easy to get into a pattern of thinking that gardening is about controlling the world around you and creating a finessed, honed landscape that serves you in exactly the way you like. For me, the magic comes when I remember that I can create a landscape that serves everyone and everything. If I don't weed every intruder out, I'm giving those weed species a chance to grow and have a life. To have fed all my strawberries to the mouse I never see gives me real deep hope, and a sense of well-being. To know that I have made a contribution. That my endeavours as

a gardener have fed and nourished the world around me in some small way. For me that feels like one of the best, most enriching and most productive way to spend my time and energy.

I have big ideas for what comes next. Too many. In many ways, I suppose I have run before I can walk this year – just to get something in the ground and feel like I was achieving. I have committed the error, against my own advice, of not allowing enough time for observation. But I have bought myself time. If I do nothing next year there will still be wilderness, life and, I hope, a tangled kind of beauty. The big achievement is the greenhouse, but it now requires balance. Some other bold, square, large features elsewhere to bring some cohesion and counter its bulk. I don't know how or where that will come from, but I am jotting down ideas for the shape the garden may take when they come to me. I know it will all be reclaimed, I know it will be sustainable, recycled and wildlife welcoming and I'm getting a sense that it might be lawn-less, and geometric, or completely plant-filled: a proper prairie for me to nest in, and to grow in. Watch this space.

Potential future layout #1

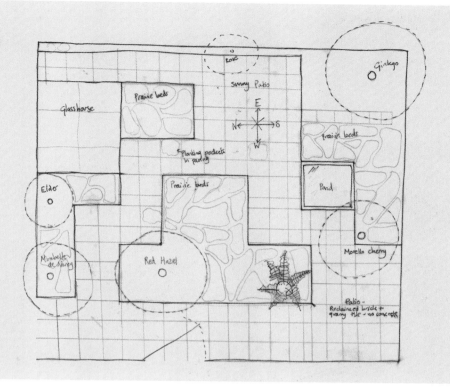

Glasshouse
Prairie beds
Rose
Sunny Patio
Ginkgo
Prairie beds
Planting pockets in paving
Prairie beds
Pond
Elder
Mirabelle de Nancy
Red Hazel
Morello cherry
Patio – Reclaimed brick + quarry tile - no concrete

Potential future layout #2

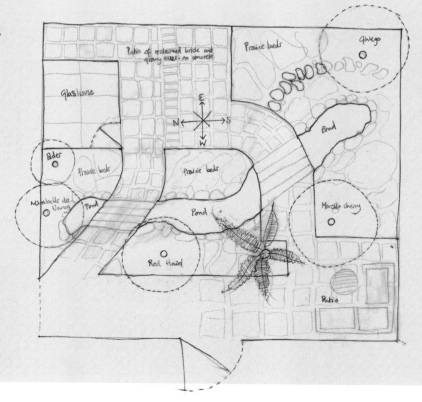

Patio of reclaimed brick and quarry tiles - no concrete
Prairie beds
Ginkgo
Glasshouse
Pond
Elder
Prairie beds
Prairie beds
Mirabelle de Nancy
Pond
Pond
Morello cherry
Red Hazel
Patio

Index

Note: page numbers in **bold** refer to information contained in captions.